short-cut rhodes

SHORT-CUT RHODES

Gary Rhodes

Food Photographs by Sandra Lane
Photographs of Gary Rhodes by Craig Easton

BBC Books

For my sons Samuel and George

Published by BBC Books,
an imprint of BBC Worldwide Publishing,
BBC Worldwide Ltd, Woodlands,
80 Wood Lane, London W12 0TT

First published 1997
© Gary Rhodes 1997
The moral right of the author has been asserted.

The recipes in this book have been adapted from those in *Rhodes Around Britain*, *More Rhodes Around Britain* and *Open Rhodes Around Britain*.

ISBN 0 563 38343 7

Recipes tested by Debbie Major
Designed by Isobel Gillan
Food photographs by Sandra Lane
Photographs of Gary Rhodes by Craig Easton
Styling by Mary Norden
Food prepared by Gary Rhodes

Set in Bembo, and Gill Sans
Printed and bound in Great Britain by Butler & Tanner, Frome and London
Colour separations by Radstock Reproductions Ltd, Midsomer Norton
Jacket and printed paper case printed by Lawrence Allen Ltd,
 Weston-super-Mare

PREVIOUS PAGE:

Alternative Jaffa Cake Pudding (p.116)

contents

introduction

What does 'short cut' mean? To find the answer, I consulted a dictionary. *The New Collins Concise English Dictionary* gives two explanations: 1) a route that is shorter than the usual one 2) a means of saving time and effort.

Short-cut Rhodes carries both explanations, giving you easier cooking routes that will save you plenty of time and effort. Cooking a meal is rather like a car journey. If you're driving on a long trip and decide to take one or two short cuts to get you to your destination just that little bit quicker, it's only worth it if you end up in the right town. I feel exactly the same way about recipes. It is only worth taking short cuts if you reach the right end result in terms of taste, texture and flavours.

If someone had suggested short cuts to me many years ago I would have told them there are no such thing. I'm sure my answer would have been that if you cut the time and the number of techniques, you must also be cutting out the some of the textures and flavours. And to a point that is true, otherwise the finer details of recipes would be a waste of time. Good cooking does need those details: home-made stocks undoubtedly give sauces an added strength of flavour, and using the right ingredients maximizes the flavours of every dish. Perfection takes time and effort.

The ideas for these short-cut recipes came to me while I was writing and filming the three Rhodes books and series. I have been fortunate, while travelling around the UK, to have met so many people who've given me their cooking tips. You may have noticed in the last two books in particular that I have given lots of variations to my recipes. This is because I wanted you to experience the maximum taste and flavours of every dish. In fact, one of my first short cuts appeared in the Lemon Soufflé recipe in *Open Rhodes around Britain* and I've featured an even shorter version here (see p.106).

The recipes in this book have been carefully selected and aim to get you almost as close to perfection as the originals. Working on *Short-cut Rhodes* has been a pleasant surprise because the dishes still taste so good and there's a great sense of achievement in that you get good home-made cooking in quick-march time. It was this home-made quality that gave me the inspiration for this book. We usually find 'home-made' written on jars of jam or pickle at a local fair and we buy them because we know we're getting something special that's very different from the commercially produced brands. For most of us nowadays, the time to cook good food at home every day just isn't there. Sunday lunch is often the only family meal that is freshly cooked. I hope these recipes will make Sundays even easier and tempt you into finding more than one Sunday in your week.

Almost every recipe in this book has variations or Extra Rhodes. These will help you to find additional flavours, so if you've run out of ideas simply turn to the ends of the recipes for inspiration. The guiding principle of the book has been to keep every avenue open so you can explore the possibilities, work at full speed and accelerate the tastes and flavours of your cooking on any day of the week. I hope I've done just that. Enjoy your travels!

notes on ingredients and techniques

- **Fresh white breadcrumbs.** In some recipes I have given specific amounts, but in most cases I have suggested that you take medium-thick slices of white bread, remove the crusts and then make them into crumbs. The best and easiest way of doing this is to give the bread a quick blitz in a food processor but if you don't have one then you can achieve acceptable results doing it by hand instead. One medium-thick slice of bread will give you 25 g (1 oz) of breadcrumbs.

- **Butter.** I have stipulated unsalted butter in the recipes where I think it works best but if you do not have any, don't worry too much – lightly salted butter or even ordinary salted butter will be perfectly acceptable. By a 'knob' of butter I mean just under 15 g (½ oz).

- **Eggs.** Where the size of the egg is crucial to the recipe I have recommended which size to use. Where it doesn't really matter, I have left the choice up to you.

- **Herbs.** In most cases I have used fresh herbs because of their superior and fresher taste, but frozen dried herbs, available from larger supermarkets, can be used in place of fresh ones in the sauces on p.55–7.

- **Wine.** It is always better to use the best quality wine that you can afford. You will then be able to enjoy drinking the other half of the bottle too! If the wine is very dry, add a good pinch of sugar to it before using.

- **Deep-frying.** In recipes where you need to deep-fry any foods, I have listed cooking oil in the ingredients. By this I mean sunflower or vegetable oil, not olive oil, as its flavour is far too strong. If you have a thermostatically controlled fryer then all the better, but if not, and you have to use an ordinary pan instead, it is important not to overfill the pan with oil. I always use a large pan because it allows more room in which to cook the foods. Pour about 10 cm (4 in) of oil into the pan, but do not fill it by any more than one-third or you will risk the chance of it overflowing when you lower in the food. It is best to measure the temperature using a thermometer but if you do not have one, a good gauge is to drop in a large cube of crustless white bread. It will rise to the surface and turn an attractive golden brown in about 2 minutes for 170°C/325°F, 1½ minutes for 180°C/350°F and 1 minute for 190°C/375°F.

■ **Stocks and sauces.** A good stock is the base of a well-flavoured gravy or sauce. Obviously in a professional kitchen, we spend hours making stocks, but cooking at home is a completely different story. Good-quality stock cubes, such as those produced by Knorr, are ideal but I do find that they need to be diluted with 600 ml (1 pint) of water, rather than the recommended smaller amount, otherwise they tend to be a little over-salty. Some supermarkets now also sell small pots of fresh stock, so with those you don't even have to boil the kettle.

I have found that Madeira Wine Gravy and White Wine Gravy in Crosse & Blackwell's Bonne Cuisine range form an excellent base for many sauces. They are available in all major supermarkets. I dilute the mix with 450 ml (¾ pint) of water rather than the recommended 300 ml (10 fl oz). You can, of course, use a gravy of your choice if you prefer.

notes on the recipes

1 Follow one set of measurements only; do not mix metric and imperial.
2 Wash fresh produce before preparation.
3 Spoon measurements are level.
4 A tablespoon is 15 ml; a teaspoon is 5 ml.
5 Unless otherwise stated, 'season' or 'seasoning' simply means seasoning with salt and pepper.
6 I recommend Bournville chocolate where recipes call for 'good-quality plain chocolate'.
7 Gas guns can be used to give a crispy sugar glaze to many desserts. It is important to be fully aware of how to operate and use the gun as this is not a conventional kitchen utensil. Obviously, gas guns should not be used by children.
8 Oven temperatures and cooking times are flexible and may vary according to the equipment and ingredients used.
9 Butter and cream may be reduced, if not excluded, in most savoury recipes.
10 Ingredients are listed with the most important ingredients first, followed by the other ingredients in order of use.

starters and snacks

Cabbage, Bacon and Onion Soup (p.14)

i

f you're looking for short-cut meals, it might seem a little strange to have dishes listed as starters. Surely if it's a 'short cut' we're after, we shouldn't even be thinking of a starter! But, in fact, these 'starters' give us so many options.

Not every dish or meal we're cooking is going to need a dramatic short cut. You may well be looking for a tasty, quick starter to make your meal complete. That's just what I've got for you here.

But these dishes are not only 'starters' – every single dish can turn into a simple snack. So if it's a Sunday evening (or indeed any evening) and you can't decide what to eat, these recipes will certainly help you make up your mind. The Curried Scrambled Eggs (p.36) take minutes to make and offer sheer culinary pleasure! Served with crusty bread or crispy toast, what could be easier?

If you're not a great fan of curry, why not try Quick Cheddar Macaroni (p.40) – a great British classic made in minutes. The macaroni cheese eats so well you'll probably find that it will disappear even faster than the time it took to cook it!

These starter/snacks also work very well together for those big occasion parties or family gatherings, especially at Christmas or New Year when you want to spend time with friends and family rather than cooking. Here are some suggestions for a buffet: Short-cut Salmon Pâté (p.16), Chicken Liver Pâté (p.18), Caesar Salad (p.24), Niçoise Salad (p.26), Simple Spanish Omelette (p.34) and Quick Cheddar Macaroni (p.40). For more ideas, just turn the pages and take a closer and 'quicker' look.

quick gazpacho soup

This 'gazpacho' needs simple preparation, with just a liquidizer or food processor to make it.

Serves 6

1 x 400 g (14 oz) can red pimientos (peppers)

1 x 400 g (14 oz) can chopped tomatoes

½ Ogen or Charentais melon, halved, seeded, skinned and roughly chopped

½ cucumber, skinned, halved, seeds removed with a teaspoon and roughly chopped

50 g (2 oz) fresh white breadcrumbs

3–4 tablespoons red wine vinegar

1 garlic clove, crushed

150 ml (5 fl oz) olive oil

1 teaspoon caster sugar

salt and freshly ground black pepper

Simply blitz all the ingredients together in two batches in a food processor to a smooth, delicious soup. Chill before serving.

Extra Rhodes . . .

- *For a smoother finish, push the soup through a sieve before chilling.*
- *For an even fresher taste, make this soup with 675 g (1½ lb) of ripe, fresh tomatoes which have been quartered and had the seeds removed.*
- *This soup is traditionally served with a number of different garnishes which are added to the soup before eating. Choose one or a selection of the following: soured cream, diced tomato, diced cucumber, diced sweet peppers, bread croûtons, chopped fresh tarragon or basil.*

cabbage, bacon and onion soup

This soup stays streets ahead of all others as a good, hearty soup for winter (or any time of the year). It's very quick to make – the hardest task is slicing the cabbage. As you can see from the photo on p. 10–11, it looks colourful and appetizing and tastes even better!

Serves 6

1 small Savoy cabbage, quartered, cored and thinly shredded
25 g (1 oz) butter
3 medium onions, sliced
8 rashers of rindless smoked back bacon, cut into thin strips
1.2–1.5 litres (2–2 ½ pints) chicken stock
salt and freshly ground black pepper

1 Melt the butter in a large pan. Add the onions and cook for a few minutes over a medium heat, without colouring, until softened.

2 Add the bacon, increase the heat under the pan, and cook for 3–4 minutes until both the onions and the bacon are lightly golden.

3 Add the chicken stock and simmer for a further 3–4 minutes.

4 Bring the stock to the boil and add the sliced cabbage. Bring back to the boil and simmer for 5 minutes or until the cabbage is just tender. Check the seasoning and serve.

Extra Rhodes . . .

- *Garnish the soup with the meatballs on p. 73.*
- *For a more substantial meal, serve the soup with home-made dumplings.*
- *A knob of butter added to the soup at the end of cooking will give you a silkier finish.*

mulligatawny soup

This recipe is featured in Open Rhodes Around Britain *where there are 22 ingredients listed – and that's without the pinch of salt – so this really is a short cut! This is a great soup to make during the winter months as it can become a complete meal when served with some good crusty bread.*

Serves 4–6

1 medium baking potato, peeled and cut into rough 1 cm (½ in) dice

1 large carrot, peeled and cut into rough 1 cm (½ in) dice

1 large onion, chopped

1 leek, cleaned and sliced

2 celery sticks, sliced (optional)

25 g (1 oz) butter

1 tablespoon medium curry powder

1 teaspoon tomato purée

900 ml (1½ pints) vegetable stock

salt

1 Melt the butter in a large pan. Add the vegetables and cook for 5 minutes. Add the curry powder and cook for a further 2 minutes.

2 Add the tomato purée and stock. Bring the soup to a simmer, cover and cook for 20 minutes, until the vegetables are tender.

3 Blitz the soup in liquidizer or with a hand blender until smooth. Season with salt and serve.

Extra Rhodes . . .

- *Garnish the soup with a little cooked long-grain rice.*
- *Sweeten the flavour with a tablespoon of mango chutney before blitzing.*
- *Cook some chopped apple in the soup for a fruitier flavour.*

short-cut salmon pâté

This is a good, quick pâté that has unlimited variations. It works well with smoked or fresh salmon, smoked mackerel, smoked trout, tinned tuna, cooked peeled prawns, cooked crab or even lobster!

Serves 4

100 g (4 oz) can red or pink salmon

a squeeze of lemon juice

50 g (2 oz) unsalted butter, softened

3 tablespoons crème fraîche

salt and freshly ground black pepper

1 Remove any skin and bones from the salmon, if necessary.

2 Place the fish and any liquid from the tin in a food processor with the lemon juice. Blitz for a few seconds until smooth.

3 Add the butter and blitz again. Stir in the crème fraîche and season with salt and pepper. Serve immediately or chill for a slightly firmer texture.

Extra Rhodes . . .

- *This pâté can also be rolled into a cylinder in some clingfilm, chilled and then cut into slices to serve.*
- *If you are making this pâté some time in advance, spoon it into individual ramekins or a larger bowl and cover with a thin layer of melted butter before chilling to seal in the flavour.*
- *For an extra spicy flavour, add a pinch of cayenne pepper, a teaspoon of English or Dijon mustard or a teaspoon of horseradish cream (or all three!).*

tuna and almond cream toasts

This garlic and almond cream base can also be flavoured with other canned fish or meat, such as salmon, chopped cooked ham or bacon. The 'toasts' can be slices of bread, but I often sit it on top of crusty French bread or rolls.

Serves 2–4
225 g (8 oz) can tuna in brine or oil

2 slices white bread, soaked in water

2 garlic cloves, crushed

6 tablespoons mayonnaise

50 g (2 oz) ground almonds

a pinch of salt

4 slices white or wholemeal bread or halved bread rolls, to serve

1 Pre-heat the grill to medium. Squeeze the excess water from the bread. Put it into a food processor with the crushed garlic and blitz for a few seconds until smooth.

2 Transfer to a bowl and stir in the mayonnaise, ground almonds and salt.

3 Drain the canned tuna and break it into flakes. Fold into the 'cream' mix.

4 Lightly toast the bread until golden. The 'cream' mix can now be spread on top and returned under the grill for a few minutes, until heated through and glazed to a golden brown.

Extra Rhodes . . .

- *A few drops of soy sauce or lemon juice can be added to the mix.*
- *These toasts eat well with a watercress salad.*

chicken liver pâté

This really is easy and quick to make. It is best made with fresh chicken livers, but frozen ones will also work. Then all you need is some hot, thick toast to spread it on!

Serves 4

225 g (8 oz) chicken livers, trimmed of any sinews

100 g (4 oz) butter, softened

1 large shallot, very finely chopped OR 1 tablespoon finely chopped onion

1 garlic clove, crushed

1–2 tablespoons brandy (optional)

salt and freshly ground black pepper

1 Melt a large knob of the butter in a frying-pan. Season the livers, then add them to the pan with the shallot or onion and garlic and fry over a high heat for 3–4 minutes, until firm but still pink in the middle. Remove from the pan and leave to cool.

2 Place the cold chicken livers in a food processor and blitz until smooth, or push through a sieve. Mix in the remaining butter and brandy, if using, check the seasoning and place into a bowl or mould. Chill before serving.

Extra Rhodes . . .

- *If you are making this pâté a day or two in advance, then it is best to top it with a very thin layer of melted butter. Once the pâté is refrigerated, this will seal in its flavours and freshness.*
- *Add a dash of Tabasco sauce or Worcestershire sauce to lift the overall flavour of the pâté.*
- *Fold 50–75 ml (2–3 fl oz) of lightly whipped double cream into the pâté for a softer, richer taste.*

devilled fish fingers

These are deep-fried, which will be very easy if you have a deep-fat fryer, but if not, don't worry. The 'deep-frying' can simply be done in 1 cm (½ in) of oil in a large frying-pan.

Serves 4   450 g (1 lb) fish fillets, such as herring, mackerel, plaice or sole, skinned

4 teaspoons cayenne pepper

½ teaspoon salt

8 tablespoons plain flour

8 tablespoons milk

cooking oil, for deep-frying

1 Cut the fish into 1 cm (½ in) strips. Heat the oil to 180°C/350°F (see p.8).

2 Mix the cayenne pepper and salt with the flour. Dip the 'fingers' into the milk and then the flour, making sure that they all get an even coating.

3 Drop half the fingers into the hot oil and cook for 1½–2 minutes until golden and crispy. Lift out with a slotted spoon on to plenty of kitchen paper and shake off the excess oil. Cook the rest in the same way. Season with a little more salt before serving, if you wish.

- *These fingers eat very well with soured cream or mayonnaise.*
- *They can also be made with thin strips of chicken breast fillet – just cook them for 2–3 minutes.*
- *Use raw peeled tiger prawns instead of fish fillets and cook for 1½ minutes.*
- *Remove the skin from 450 g (1 lb) of sausages. Roll the meat into walnut-sized balls (2–3 from each sausage), roll through the milk and flour and deep-fry a few at a time for 3–4 minutes until golden. Serve on cocktail sticks with the soured cream, mayonnaise or a spicy tomato relish as an appetizer.*

prawn or crab dumplings

These are delicious with Lemon Butter Sauce (p.55) or as a garnish for a fish soup.

Makes 4 large or 8 smaller dumplings	100 g (4 oz) cooked peeled prawns OR drained canned white crab meat
	100 g (4 oz) fresh white breadcrumbs
	2 tablespoons double cream
	1 egg
	1 egg yolk
	a pinch of freshly grated nutmeg
	a knob of butter
	2 tablespoons cooking oil
	salt and freshly ground black pepper
	lemon or lime wedges or soured cream, to serve

1 Blitz the prawns or crab, breadcrumbs, cream, egg, egg yolk, grated nutmeg, seasoning in a food processor until well mixed. Check the seasoning, transfer to a bowl, cover and chill for 1 hour.

2 Mould the mixture into 4 large or 8 smaller balls, then lightly flatten them into 2 cm (¾ in) thick discs.

3 Heat the butter and oil in a large frying-pan. Fry the dumplings over a medium heat for 3–4 minutes each side until golden all over. Serve with a wedge of lemon or lime or a dot of soured cream.

Extra Rhodes . . .

- *For a sauce to serve with the dumplings, heat 6 tablespoons of canned crab or lobster bisque with a splash of single cream, a squeeze of lemon juice and a little brandy or white wine if you wish.*
- *For a soup garnish, cook the dumplings in simmering water or fish stock; 8–10 minutes for the large ones or 6–8 minutes for the small ones.*

SALADS and dressings

I'm a great fan of good salads. They can be as simple as a bowl of green leaves tossed with a good dressing. So many salad dressings can be bought ready-made, but for me the flavours often taste too artificial when just a few drops of good olive oil is all the salad really needs. Here are a couple of speedy salads, a simple salad dressing, and a spicy tomato dressing that works equally well mixed with warm pasta or rice as a vegetarian dish.

caesar salad

Serves 4

2 cos OR 6 little gem lettuces

For the Caesar dressing:

1 tablespoon mayonnaise

15 g (½ oz) canned anchovy fillets, drained

2 teaspoons capers

1 teaspoon Dijon mustard

juice of ½ lemon

2 tablespoons freshly grated Parmesan

150 ml (5 fl oz) olive oil

freshly ground black pepper

1 Break the lettuce leaves into small pieces and wash them well in cold water. Drain and then dry the leaves well – a salad spinner does this brilliantly.

2 For the dressing, put the mayonnaise, anchovies, capers, mustard, lemon juice, Parmesan and some pepper into a liquidizer and blitz until smooth. Pour into a bowl and gradually whisk in the oil until you have a loose, creamy consistency.

3 Toss the dressing with the salad leaves and serve immediately.

Extra Rhodes . . .

- *Add ½ crushed garlic clove, a dash of Tabasco sauce and 1–2 teaspoons of Worcestershire sauce to the dressing for a spicier taste.*
- *Toss extra Parmesan, snipped anchovy fillets and toasted or fried croûtons into the leaves after dressing.*

basic salad dressing

This is sufficient to dress 1 large lettuce.

Serves 4
65 ml (2½ fl oz) olive oil

juice of ½ lemon
salt and freshly ground black pepper

Simply whisk the oil with the lemon juice and some seasoning.

Extra Rhodes...

- *Replace half the olive oil with groundnut, hazelnut or walnut oil.*
- *Use one of the following in place of lemon juice: fresh lime juice, balsamic vinegar, red or white wine vinegar, herb-flavoured or fruit-flavoured vinegar.*

- *Add 3 teaspoons of Dijon or English mustard to the vinegar before whisking in the oil for a thin, mayonnaise-style dressing.*
- *Flavour with some freshly crushed garlic, horseradish sauce or pesto.*
- *Stir in one of the following: a little finely chopped shallot or onion, diced tomato, chopped fresh herbs, sliced spring onions, mustard seeds or chopped olives or chillies.*

spicy tomato dressing

This is sufficient to dress 2 large lettuces or to coat 225 g (8 oz) cooked pasta or rice.

Serves 4
3 tablespoons tomato ketchup
1½ tablespoons white wine vinegar
½ tablespoon Worcestershire sauce

a dash of Tabasco sauce
65 ml (2½ fl oz) olive oil
salt and freshly ground black pepper

1 Mix together the ketchup, wine vinegar, Worcestershire sauce and Tabasco sauce.

2 Whisk in the olive oil and season with salt and pepper if needed.

niçoise salad

Here's a salad that will really help turn a can of tuna into something quite special.
It eats well with some good oven-baked garlic bread.

Serves 4

225 g (8 oz) can tuna

I large, crisp green lettuce, broken into small pieces OR
   a large bag of prepared mixed salad leaves

2 tomatoes, each cut into 8

100 g (4 oz) cooked green beans

8–10 cooked new potatoes, quartered

2 hard-boiled eggs, quartered

For the dressing:

3 tablespoons olive oil

½ teaspoon Dijon mustard

I tablespoon white wine or tarragon vinegar

salt and freshly ground black pepper

1 Drain the can of tuna and break the fish into large flakes. Break the lettuce into small pieces, then wash and dry it well.

2 Place the lettuce, tomatoes, beans and potatoes in a large bowl.

3 Seal all the dressing ingredients in a glass jar and give it a good shake. Add to the salad bowl and toss everything together.

4 Add the tuna and lightly toss together once more, trying not to break up the pieces of fish too much. Arrange the eggs in the salad and serve.

Extra Rhodes . . .

- *Add black olives, capers and anchovy fillets to the salad ingredients.*
- *Add crushed garlic and chopped fresh tarragon or chives to the dressing.*

spinach, onion and cheddar cheese mushrooms

These mushrooms (illustrated on p.30) are great as a starter or a main course. If you are serving them as a main course, then it's best to use really large, flat mushrooms so that you will only need one per person. The smaller, flat open-cup mushrooms are ideal for starters and as a vegetable accompaniment.

Serves 4

450 g (1 lb) fresh spinach OR 350 g (12 oz) frozen leaf spinach, thawed and drained well

4 large flat mushrooms OR 12 smaller open-cup mushrooms, stalks removed

olive or cooking oil

15 g (½ oz) butter

2 small onions, thinly sliced

100 g (4 oz) grated Cheddar OR cheese slices

salt and freshly ground black pepper

1 If you are using fresh spinach, wash it thoroughly, shake off the excess water and pack it into a large pan. Stir and cook over a high heat for about 2 minutes until it has wilted to the bottom of the pan. Drain and coarsely chop.

2 Pre-heat the grill to medium. Lay the mushrooms rounded-side down on a lightly greased baking sheet. Season with salt and pepper and then trickle over a little oil.

3 Cook the mushrooms under the grill until tender, 7–8 minutes for the larger mushrooms and 4–5 minutes for the smaller ones.

4 Melt the butter in a frying-pan. Slice the mushroom stalks and add to the pan with the onions. Increase the heat under the pan and allow the onions to soften and become golden brown.

5 Stir the spinach into the onions and allow to heat through. Season with salt and pepper.

6 Spoon the mixture on top of the mushrooms and cover with the cheese. Simply finish by melting the cheese under the grill.

Extra Rhodes . . .

The following can all be finished with cheese on top.
- *Drizzle the mushrooms with garlic butter instead of oil before cooking.*
- *Cook some chopped bacon or leeks with the onions.*
- *Top the mushrooms with rarebit mix (see p.32) instead of the grated cheese.*
- *Top the mushrooms with home-made or canned ratatouille.*
- *Top with the cooked onions, sliced tomato and chopped basil.*
- *Top with cooked minced lamb, fried aubergine slices moussaka-style.*
- *Top with bolognese sauce and then cheese (perhaps Parmesan).*
- *Top with cooked peeled prawns drizzled with garlic butter.*
- *Serve either type of mushroom with a ready-made tomato sauce.*

OVERLEAF

Left: Spinach, Onion and Cheddar Cheese Mushrooms (p.28)

Right: Baked Potato and Onion Rarebit (p.32)

WELSH RAREBIT and all its friends

Welsh Rarebit is certainly a great British classic that, once made, will give you plenty of alternatives for different dishes. The real advantage of the rarebit mixture is that it will keep refrigerated for up to 10 days and also freezes brilliantly, making it ideal for impromptu meals.

basic welsh rarebit mix

Although this mix can be used as a topping for all types of dishes,
it stands on its own as the classic topping for toast.

Make 8–10 portions
350 g (12 oz) Cheddar
85 ml (3 fl oz) milk
25 g (1 oz) plain flour
25 g (1 oz) fresh white breadcrumbs

½ tablespoon English mustard powder
a few shakes of Worcestershire sauce
1 egg
1 egg yolk
slices of bread or halved bread rolls, to serve

1 Put the cheese and milk into a pan and slowly melt together. Add the flour, breadcrumbs and mustard and cook for a few minutes until the mixture leaves the sides of the pan. Add the Worcestershire sauce and leave to cool.

2 Once cold, scrape the mix into a food processor. With the machine running, slowly add the egg and the egg yolk. If a processor is unavailable, then simply beat in by hand. The rarebit mix is now made and is best left to chill for 1 hour before using, or dividing into smaller quantities and freezing.

3 To cook, pre-heat the grill to high. Toast the slices of bread on both sides until lightly golden. Mould some of the rarebit with your hands to fit the shape of the toasted bread. Rest it on top and then slide it back under the grill for a few minutes until glazed to golden brown.

Extra Rhodes . . .

These ideas will suit starters, snacks and main courses:
- *Mix the rarebit with flakes of kipper and cook as before. Serve with a poached egg.*
- *Use the mix to finish a potato-topped fish, cottage or shepherd's pie.*

- Use to cover cooked broccoli or cauliflower as a snack or vegetable.
- Use to top cooked burgers, sausages or patties (see p.73).
- And to summarize, use to top: chicken, fish, pies, flans, pizzas, pastas, vegetables, potatoes and more!

- Make it into Stilton rarebit on toast by replacing one-third or half of the Cheddar with some Stilton (how much will depend on its strength). Serve as an after-dinner course with sticks of celery and a watercress salad.

baked potato and onion rarebit

This makes a wonderful snack with a tomato or mixed leaf salad, or simply on its own (as illustrated on p.31).

Serves 4
2 large baking potatoes
50 g (2 oz) butter
1 bunch of spring onions, trimmed and sliced thinly

2 tablespoons soured cream
175 g (6 oz) rarebit mix (see opposite)
salt and freshly ground black pepper

1 Pre-heat the oven to 200°C/400°F/gas 6. Bake the potatoes for approximately 1 hour or until tender. Pre-heat the grill to high.

2 Melt 25 g (1 oz) of the butter in a pan, add the spring onions and cook gently for a minute or two until just softened.

3 Halve the potatoes lengthways and spoon most of the potato into a bowl, saving the skins to finish the dish. Fork in the rest of the butter and some salt and pepper, then fold in the spring onions and soured cream.

4 The potato mix can now be spooned back into the skins. Divide the rarebit mix into 4 and sit on top of each potato. These can now be finished to a golden brown and a delicious texture under the grill.

Extra Rhodes . . .

- Add more soured cream or 1–2 tablespoons of olive oil for a richer finish.
- Stir some cooked mushrooms, ratatouille or spinach into the potato mix.

simple spanish omelette

A traditional Spanish omelette is normally made from thinly sliced potatoes cooked in the pan with some onions. That's very easy, but this version makes it even easier by using left-over cooked potatoes, whether they are boiled, roasted, old or new.

Serves 2–4
4 eggs, beaten

450 g (1 lb) cooked potatoes, sliced

a knob of butter

1 large onion, sliced

salt and freshly ground black pepper

1 Melt the butter in a 20 cm (8 in) non-stick frying-pan. Add the onion and cook over a medium heat for a few minutes, without colouring, until soft.

2 Add the potatoes and continue to fry until they are heated through. Season with salt and pepper.

3 Lower the heat slightly, pour the beaten eggs on top and stir lightly with a fork to give an even cooking of the eggs. As it begins to thicken, stop stirring and allow the omelette to colour on the base.

4 Invert the omelette on to a plate. Slide it back into the pan for 1–2 minutes to colour on the other side. Cut like a cake to serve.

Extra Rhodes . . .

- *Fry sliced red, green or yellow peppers or mushrooms with the onions.*
- *Don't turn the omelette during cooking. Simply cover with sliced tomatoes and grated cheese and finish under the grill until golden and bubbling.*
- *This eats very well with fried sliced red pepper dressed with olive oil, lemon juice, salt and pepper (see photograph opposite).*

curried scrambled eggs

Here's a quick snack recipe that eats really well with warm naan bread and a good tossed salad. I've also included some other flavours and ingredients, which can be added to make this dish even more tasty and exciting, so now you can have it for dinner, lunch or even a spicy breakfast.

Serves 1

3 eggs, beaten

a knob of butter

1 heaped tablespoon finely chopped onion

¼ teaspoon mild curry powder

a pinch of salt

a pinch of sugar (optional)

1 Heat a small frying-pan over a medium heat, add the butter and leave to melt. Add the onion and cook, without colouring, for 2–3 minutes.

2 Add the curry powder to the onions and continue to cook for a couple of minutes.

3 Pour on the eggs and season with the salt and sugar, if using. The sugar will obviously give you a slightly sweeter curry flavour.

4 Stir the eggs until they have softly scrambled. Your curried eggs are now ready to serve.

Extra Rhodes . . .

- *Cook ¼ teaspoon of crushed garlic and ¼ teaspoon of finely grated fresh ginger with the onion.*
- *Fry some diced cooked potato with the onion.*
- *Cook a few sliced mushrooms or some sliced red or green pepper with the onion, before adding the eggs.*

To the finished eggs:
- *Stir in some chopped tomato.*
- *Stir in some chopped fresh coriander.*
- *Add a drop of soured cream or natural yoghurt.*
- *Add a little bit of mango chutney.*

salmon fish cakes

Here's a quick alternative to one of my most popular dishes.

Serves 4
225 g (8 oz) can pink or red salmon, drained and liquid reserved

225 g (8 oz) mashed potatoes

a squeeze of fresh lemon juice

plain flour, for coating

1 egg, beaten

75 g (3 oz) dried golden or fresh white breadcrumbs

cooking oil, for deep-frying

salt and freshly ground black pepper

lemon wedges and Quick Tartare Sauce (see p.57), to serve

1 Remove any skin and bones from the salmon. Break the fish into flakes and mix with the potatoes. Add the lemon and season. Add a few teaspoons of the fish liquid for a richer flavour, if you wish.

2 Shape into large or walnut-sized balls and coat with flour. Dip into the beaten egg and then the breadcrumbs. Coat once more in egg and breadcrumbs for a thicker, crunchier finish.

3 Heat the oil in a deep-fat fryer to 180°C/350°F (see p.8) and cook for 4–5 minutes, until golden. Serve with lemon and tartare sauce.

Extra Rhodes . . .

- *Boil 1 chopped onion in 120 ml (4 fl oz) of white wine until almost dry. Cool and add to the mixture with 2 teaspoons of chopped parsley or tarragon.*
- *Shape into 4 discs and cook in a frying pan with a knob of butter and 2–3 tablespoons cooking oil over a medium heat for 3 minutes on each side until golden.*

quick cheddar macaroni

A great tea or supper dish, macaroni cheese is ideal for all the family. We take it to the table with some crusty bread and a green salad and then all dig in! One of the beauties of it is its simplicity, and this is the extra speedy version.

Serves 4–6
350 g (12 oz) dried or fresh macaroni
600 ml (1 pint) milk
25 g (1 oz) cornflour
175 g (6 oz) Cheddar, grated
1 teaspoon Dijon or English mustard
salt and freshly ground black pepper

1 Cook dried macaroni according to the packet instructions. Cook fresh macaroni in boiling salted water for 4–5 minutes until tender. Drain and set aside.

2 Pre-heat the grill to medium. Mix 120 ml (4 fl oz) of the milk with the cornflour. Bring the remaining milk to the boil and then whisk in the cornflour mixture, a little at a time, until a good, thick white sauce is attained. Simmer for 4–5 minutes, stirring occasionally.

3 Add 100 g (4 oz) of the cheese and the mustard to the pan and allow the cheese to melt into the sauce. Season with salt and pepper. If it is in any way lumpy, strain it through a sieve on to the macaroni and mix well.

4 Spoon into a serving dish and sprinkle with the remaining grated cheese. This can now be finished under a hot grill until golden brown.

- Stir in some cooked sliced onions or leeks.
- Spice up the sauce with a little Tabasco or Worcestershire sauce.
- Replace half the Cheddar with grated Stilton for 'blue' macaroni!
- Use the cheese sauce with cooked fish, cauliflower, broccoli, spinach or other vegetables.
- For non-vegetarians, add some chopped pieces of cooked bacon.
- For a richer sauce, replace 150 ml (5 fl oz) of the milk with single cream.

main courses

Roast Leg of Lamb with
Boulangère Potatoes (p.84)

*t*his chapter covers virtually all cooking methods, from pan-frying and grilling to stewing and braising. The short cut with the stewing and braising methods really comes in the initial preparation – for example, in the Beef and Mushroom Stew on p.76, you'll find that the sauce-making is finished at the very end of cooking (and it only takes minutes!). This obviously makes the dish a lot easier and the short cut removes all the care and attention usually needed to prevent it from sticking. The stew basically looks after itself.

One easy short cut given in the variation at the end of the recipe – and also in a variation for Bacon in the Pot on p.82 – is to use a pressure cooker. This cuts the cooking time by two-thirds.

You'll also find recipes for meat sauces that can be made to liven up almost any cooked meat dish – whether it's a steak, chop or cutlet. Red wine, *au poivre*, *chasseur* and other sauces are very easy to make and lift a simple steak or chop to new heights.

How about a short-cut vegetarian dish? The crispy Aubergine Toast 'Pizzas' (p.50) are great fun and a tasty dish to try. The crispy base is simply toast, topped with grilled aubergines, a rich tomato sauce and melting cheese. It's quick to make and brings a new meaning to 'Pizza Express'!

Let's move on to fish, which is one of my favourite foods. Lots of fresh fish are available to us from local fishmongers and now almost every supermarket has a huge range on display. I have included Deep-fried Cod in Batter (p.58) and Baked Haddock with a Parsley Crust (p.60) among others for you to try.

Fish should always be cooked as simply as possible, so as not to mask the wonderful fresh taste. It cooks quickly, keeping the flakes succulent and tender, which makes it a perfect main ingredient for easy-to-prepare meals.

The flavours I'm suggesting here simply help to enhance the natural flavour of the fish itself.

I love to eat a whole grilled plaice or sole just topped with a flavoured melting butter (see p.55 and 56). For me it's a complete meal, accompanied by crusty bread to soak up the butter. To help you cook fish, I've included some tips and times for different fish types.

There's also a chicken dish here that I would love you all to try: my Chicken Curry (see p.64). It really couldn't be any easier and quicker. Have you ever made a chicken curry in 15–20 minutes? This has to be a bonus; the curry cooks almost as quickly as the rice. And the main ingredient apart from the chicken? A can of evaporated milk. At the expense of repeating myself, I have to say it's so easy!

So which dishes have you seen and tried so far? A salad? Chicken curry? How do your fancy a soufflé to finish? Yes, it's a short cut and you'll find it with other tasty sweet puds on p.88. See you there!

pasta with mushrooms

Use your favourite pasta for this dish and enough cream to bind all the flavours.

Serves 4

350 g (12 oz) dried pasta, cooked

350 g (12 oz) mushrooms, sliced

25 g (1 oz) butter

2 tablespoons olive oil

1 onion, finely chopped

1 garlic clove, crushed (optional)

150 ml (5 fl oz) single cream

50 g (2 oz) finely grated Parmesan (optional)

salt and freshly ground black pepper

flatleaf parsley, chopped (optional)

1 Melt the butter with the oil in a pan. Add the onion and garlic, if using, and cook for a few minutes until softened, without colouring.

2 Turn up the heat, add the mushrooms and cook for a few minutes, until just softened. Add the cream and simmer for a few minutes.

3 Add the pasta and toss gently over a low heat until heated through. Fold in the Parmesan, season with salt and pepper, sprinkle with chopped parsley, if using, and serve.

Extra Rhodes . . .

- *Use button, chestnut, field or wild mushrooms.*
- *Add a squeeze of lemon juice to the sauce to lift all the flavours.*
- *Stir some chopped cooked ham or bacon into the finished sauce.*
- *Add some cooked sweet peppers, broad beans or peas.*
- *Pour the finished dish into a shallow ovenproof dish, sprinkle with more Parmesan or Cheddar and glaze under the grill.*

parmesan risotto

There's no real way of taking any short cuts with risotto apart from making the recipe as simple as possible without compromising on the flavour, as I've done here. The good thing is that risottos are a great short cut to a complete meal! There are two rules that, if kept to, mean you just can't go wrong. The first is to use arborio rice and the second is to always make sure the stock is hot. Here's a basic recipe for a Parmesan risotto. Then check out the ideas opposite for how to change it to the flavour of your choice.

Serves 4

225 g (8 oz) arborio rice

100 g (4 oz) unsalted butter

1 tablespoon olive oil

2 large onions, finely chopped

1.2 litres (2 pints) chicken, fish or vegetable stock

2–4 tablespoons finely grated Parmesan

salt and freshly ground black pepper

1 Melt 75 g (3 oz) of the butter with the olive oil in a large pan. Add the chopped onions and cook gently, without colouring, for a few minutes, until soft. Meanwhile, bring the stock to a simmer in another pan.

2 Add the rice to the onions and continue to cook, stirring, for a few minutes.

3 Add the hot stock to the rice a ladleful at a time, allowing the risotto to simmer gently. Once the stock has been absorbed by the rice, add another ladleful.

4 Continue this process, stirring almost continuously, to keep an even cooking and prevent the rice from sticking. The risotto will take 20–25 minutes to cook. Make sure there is still a very slight bite left in the rice at the end as this prevents it from becoming too starchy and almost puddingy.

5 Add the Parmesan to taste and the remaining 25 g (1 oz) of butter to give the risotto a creamier finish. Once the cheese has been added, a drop more stock may well be needed as the cheese will thicken the consistency. Season with salt and pepper and it's ready!

Extra Rhodes . . .

Parmesan is a flavour I never leave out of a risotto. It's a predominant one, which lifts so many others, so do leave it in for all the additions below.

- *Stir strips of cooked bacon into the finished risotto.*
- *Add some chopped fresh herbs, such as parsley, tarragon and basil.*
- *Stir in some chopped cooked spinach.*
- *Cook some seeded and chopped fresh chillies with the onions.*
- *Fry some red and green peppers with the onions.*
- *Cook 225 g (8 oz) of mushrooms with the onions.*
- *Stir some diced and fried black pudding into a finished basic or mushroom risotto.*
- *Add 1 leek, finely shredded, towards the end of cooking.*
- *Add 225 g (8 oz) of cooked peeled prawns or white crab meat towards the end of cooking. Also, half a can of lobster or crab bisque can be added at the end to give a rich shellfish finish.*
- *Replace half the quantity of stock with 1 can of chopped tomatoes, together with all the liquor, for a full, rich tomato and Parmesan flavour.*
- *Halve the quantity of butter in the recipe for a less rich finish.*

aubergine toast 'pizzas'

This short-cut pizza eats very well with a simple tossed green salad.

Serves 4

2 medium aubergines

1 large onion, finely chopped

1 large garlic clove, crushed

olive oil

1 x 400 g (14 oz) can chopped tomatoes, preferably with basil

2 teaspoons tomato purée or ketchup

4 thick slices crusty bread (a round loaf gives a better-shaped pizza)

175 g (6 oz) Cheddar, grated

salt and freshly ground black pepper

1 For the sauce, cook the onion and garlic in 1 tablespoon of oil for a few minutes until soft but not coloured. Add the tomatoes and purée or ketchup and simmer to a thick, chunky sauce. Season.

2 Meanwhile, pre-heat the grill to high. Cut each aubergine lengthways into 4 or 6 thick slices, brush with olive oil, season with salt and pepper and grill for a few minutes on each side, until tender. Brush the bread with a little oil and toast until golden.

3 To serve, lay the slices on top of the toast and spoon over the tomato sauce. Sprinkle with the cheese and grill until melted.

Extra Rhodes . . .

- *Choose round, crusty, white or brown, ciabatta or French bread for bases.*
- *Add 4–5 tablespoons of passata before reducing for an even richer sauce.*
- *Virtually any other flavour can be sprinkled on top of the pizzas before grilling. Choose from: sliced mushrooms, sliced sweet peppers, sweetcorn, sliced spicy sausage, peas, artichokes, anchovies, olives and so on.*

SIMPLE FISH with quick fish sauces

I love to eat good, fresh fish simply pan-fried or grilled. Eating fish doesn't always have to mean following a complicated recipe; cooking can become a lot simpler by making your main ingredient your only ingredient. I thought I would give you some general guidelines on how to cook some different types of fish and then some quick sauces to go with it, which also work well with chicken and vegetarian dishes.

pan-frying fish

This method is classically known as *à la meunière*, meaning dusted with flour, fried in butter and finished with Beurre Noisette (see p.55). All types of fish can be cooked in this way. This is my own, slightly different, method, which I find always gives me a consistent, golden brown finish.

1 Season and lightly flour the presentation side of the whole or portioned fish and then brush that side with softened butter.

2 Heat 1–2 tablespoons of cooking oil in a frying-pan.

3 Add the fish and cook until golden brown (see the timings below).

4 Now just turn over your fish and continue to fry until cooked.

Here are the cooking times for pan-frying fish over a medium heat:
- *Whole flat fish, such as plaice and sole, weighing 450–675 g (1–1½ lb): 5–6 minutes on each side*
- *Fillets of flat fish, such as plaice: 1–2 minutes on each side*
- *Whole round fish, such as mackerel and trout, weighing 350–450 g (12 oz–1 lb): 6–7 minutes on each side*

- *Round fish steaks, such as salmon and cod, weighing 175–225 g:*
  4–5 minutes on each side
- *Round fish fillet supremes (i.e. small, thick pieces of fillet) weighing about 175–225g*
  (6–8 oz): 4–5 minutes on each side

grilling fish

This has to be the simplest of cooking methods for fish. Whole flat fish and fish fillets don't need to be turned over, but whole round fish needs to be grilled on both sides (see photo overleaf).

1 Season the fish well on both sides and brush with softened butter.

2 Lay on a greased, flat baking tray or rack of the grill pan and slide under the grill until golden brown (see timings below).

3 Turn over if necessary, season and continue to grill until cooked.

Here are the cooking times for grilling fish under a medium heat:
- *Whole flat fish, such as plaice and sole, weighing 450–675 g (1–1½ lb):*
  8–10 minutes on one side only
- *Fillets of flat fish, such as plaice: 3–4 minutes on one side only*
- *Whole round fish, such as mackerel and trout, weighing 350–450 g (12 oz–1 lb):*
  5–6 minutes on each side
- *Round fish steaks, such as salmon, weighing 175–225 g (6–8 oz):*
  8–10 minutes on one side only
- *Round fish fillet supremes (i.e. small, thick pieces of fillet) weighing about 175–225 g*
  (6–8 oz): 8–10 minutes on one side only

lemon butter sauce

Serves 4–6
100 g (4 oz) chilled unsalted butter, diced
1½–2 tablespoons lemon juice

2 tablespoons well-flavoured chicken or vegetable
stock or water
salt and freshly ground black pepper

1 Simply place all the ingredients in a small pan and bring to a simmer over a low heat, whisking continuously. The sauce should not be allowed to boil as this will separate the butter. If it is a little too thick for you, add a touch more stock.

2 If you prefer a sharper taste, add a squeeze more lemon juice.

Extra Rhodes...

- *To give the sauce a creamy finish, blitz with an electric hand blender.*
- *Replace the lemon juice with lime juice.*
- *Add some chopped fresh tarragon, basil or parsley at the end.*
- *Stir finely diced tomato and chives into the sauce.*
- *Cook a little finely chopped shallot or onion in the sauce.*

nut brown butter (beurre noisette)

This is a 'sauce' which is ideal for pan-fried fish. Add the following amounts to the pan for each cooked fish.

Serves 2
a knob of butter
a squeeze of lemon juice

1 teaspoon chopped fresh parsley (optional)
salt and freshly ground black pepper

1 Once you have pan-fried your fish, remove it from the pan and pour away any oil. Add the butter and cook over a medium–high heat until it takes on a nutty brown colour.

2 Add the lemon juice, parsley, if using, and seasoning and then pour over your fish.

Opposite: Whole Grilled Plaice with Nut Brown Butter

savoury butter

The butter can be made in advance and refrigerated for 1 week or frozen for up to 2 months. It also eats well with chicken, vegetables or pasta.

Serves 4–6

3 tablespoons finely chopped onion
½ glass white wine (about 85 ml/3 fl oz)
100 g (4 oz) butter, softened
juice of 1 lemon

1 teaspoon Dijon mustard
2 tablespoons chopped fresh tarragon
2 tablespoons chopped fresh parsley
freshly ground black pepper

1 Boil the onion with the white wine until reduced and almost dry. Leave to cool.

2 Mix the wine and onions with all the remaining ingredients. Mould into a cylinder shape, wrap in clingfilm and leave to set in the fridge or freezer.

3 To use, simply slice the butter and sit it on top of the cooked fish (meat or vegetables) and allow to melt.

Extra Rhodes . . .

- *Add some finely chopped red or green chillies or a few drops of Tabasco sauce for a hotter, spicier taste.*
- *For 'Madras' butter, cook ½ teaspoon of curry powder with the onions. Replace the tarragon and parsley with fresh coriander and the lemon juice with lime.*

cream sauce

This can be made separately or in the pan in which you cooked the fish.
It also eats well with chicken and pasta.

Serves 4–6

2 tablespoons finely chopped shallots or onion

2 glasses white wine (about 250 ml/8 fl oz)

150 ml (5 fl oz) fish, chicken or vegetable stock

150 ml (5 fl oz) double cream

juice of ½ lemon

salt and freshly ground black pepper

1 Put the shallot and wine into a pan and boil until reduced by three-quarters.

2 Add the stock and reduce by half.

3 Add the cream, bring to a simmer and cook for only a few minutes. It's now time to add the lemon juice and season.

Extra Rhodes...

- *Add some chopped fresh herbs or diced tomato to the finished sauce.*
- *Cook some sliced button mushrooms with the shallots.*
- *Some grated Cheddar, Parmesan or Stilton can be stirred into the sauce.*
- *Flavour the sauce with some English or Dijon mustard, or mustard seed.*

quick tartare sauce

Using both capers and gherkins is not essential. One or the other will do the trick
(preferably capers!). This is especially good with any deep-fried fish.

Serves 4

150 ml (5 fl oz) mayonnaise

2 teaspoons chopped capers

2 teaspoons chopped gherkins

2 teaspoons finely chopped onion

a squeeze of lemon juice

salt and freshly ground black pepper

Mix all the ingredients together and serve!

deep-fried cod in batter

*My quick batter is just beer (I normally use lager, but a rich bitter would work)
mixed with self-raising flour. Just about any fish can be coated and fried, but here
the recipe is for cod fillet: the best battered fish in the world!*

Serves 4 4 × 175–225 g (6–8 oz) thick cod fillet portions, bones removed

225 g (8 oz) self-raising flour, seasoned

cooking oil, for deep-frying

300 ml (10 fl oz) lager or beer

salt and freshly ground black pepper

lemon wedges and chips, to serve

1 Season a spoonful of the flour with salt and pepper and set to one
side. Heat a deep-fat fryer or a pan of oil to 170°C/325°F (see p.8).

2 Whisk half the lager into the remaining flour, until smooth.
Continue to add the rest gradually until a thick batter is achieved.
The thicker the batter, the better the finished texture becomes.

3 Dip the cod in the flour, then in the batter and deep-fry in the
hot oil on both sides for 7–8 minutes until completely golden and
crispy. Drain briefly on kitchen paper and serve with a wedge of
lemon and a good plate of chips (oven-ready chips are easiest).

Extra Rhodes . . .

- *Use the batter to coat sausages (pork, beef or vegetarian), cocktail sausages,
  pieces of black pudding or the pork meatballs on p. 73.*
- *Cut chicken breast fillets into cubes, dip in the batter and fry for home-
  made 'chicken nuggets' that the children will love.*
- *Use the batter for coating king prawns, squid and other pieces of fish.*
- *Use the batter to coat onion rings, mushrooms, aubergines and so on.*

baked haddock WITH A PARSLEY CRUST

This breadcrumb topping can also be used to top a fish pie, a creamy chicken pie filling or a vegetarian crumble. It finishes off ratatouille beautifully, if you replace the parsley with some chopped fresh basil.

Serves 4

4 × 175–225 g (6–8 oz) haddock fillet portions, skinned

45 g (1½ oz) butter

½ small onion, very finely chopped

6 slices white bread, crusts removed and made into crumbs

2 heaped tablespoons chopped fresh parsley

salt and freshly ground black pepper

a squeeze of lemon juice or Lemon Butter Sauce (see p.55), to serve

1 Pre-heat the grill to medium. Melt the butter in a pan, add the onion and cook for 2–3 minutes, until softened, without colouring. Allow to cool slightly.

2 Mix the breadcrumbs with the 'onion butter' and chopped parsley. Season well with salt and pepper.

3 Place the pieces of haddock on a lightly buttered and seasoned baking tray. Top each piece with the parsley crumbs, pressing them on firmly to give a good crust.

4 Cook under the grill, not too near the heat, for 10–12 minutes (thin fillets may only take 8 minutes) until the fish has a milky-white texture and the crust is golden brown. Serve with just a squeeze of lemon or maybe the lemon butter sauce.

Extra Rhodes...

- *Replace the haddock with other thick white fish fillets, such as cod or hake.*
- *The dish can be lifted even more by serving on or with mashed potatoes.*
- *A mixed herb crust can be made with the addition of chopped fresh sage, basil, tarragon and thyme.*
- *Replace the chopped parsley with the finely grated zest of 1 lemon.*
- *Add a little finely grated Parmesan to the crust.*
- *Use the crust to cover lamb chops, using fresh mint in place of the parsley.*

spicy fried chicken

This recipe is for two portions which will fit neatly into a wok or frying-pan. The yoghurt marinade coagulates around the meat, giving you a dish that is stunning in flavour, texture and colour.

Serves 2

2 large chicken breast fillets, skinned and cut into thin strips or pieces

2 tablespoons natural yoghurt

juice of 1 lime

½ teaspoon turmeric

½ teaspoon paprika

a pinch of ground cardamom

1 garlic clove, crushed

a pinch of salt

1 tablespoon cooking oil

1 Mix together the yoghurt, lime juice, turmeric, paprika, cardamom, garlic and salt. Add the chicken strips and stir so that they become totally covered.

2 Heat the wok or frying-pan with 1 tablespoon of oil. When the pan is very hot, add the chicken pieces, fry for 5–6 minutes and the dish is done.

Extra Rhodes . . .

- *A squeeze of fresh lemon juice and some chopped fresh coriander add a lovely finish to this dish.*

chicken curry

This dish is featured in Open Rhodes Around Britain *as a chicken balti. In that recipe I used cardamom seeds, fresh coriander, chillies and a variety of spices. This is a very quick and few-ingredient alternative. Please promise you'll try it because it is so easy to make and tasty to eat.*

Serves 4

4–6 chicken breast fillets, diced

2 onions, chopped

1 garlic clove, crushed (optional)

3 tablespoons cooking oil

15 g (½ oz) medium curry powder (more if you prefer it hotter)

1 x 400 g (14 oz) can evaporated milk

salt and freshly ground black pepper

1 Cook the chopped onions and garlic, if using, in the oil for a few minutes, allowing them to colour slightly.

2 Add the curry powder and continue to cook for a few minutes.

3 Season the diced chicken breast with salt and pepper and add to the curried onions. Turn in the pan until completely sealed on all sides.

4 Add the evaporated milk and bring to a simmer. Cook for 15–20 minutes, stirring occasionally to prevent it sticking. Check for seasoning and your curry is ready. I told you it was quick and easy!

- *Diced cooked potato can be added for the last 5 minutes of cooking for extra texture.*
- *Buy some good naan bread to offer with it.*
- *Serve with some mango chutney and lime pickles.*
- *Eat with boiled rice, braised rice or stir-fried rice.*
- *Turn this into a vegetarian curry using onions, potatoes, courgettes, mushrooms, aubergines, carrots and so on.*
- *To lift the finished dish, sprinkle with some chopped fresh coriander.*

paprika and lemon chicken

*This idea can be used for all cuts of chicken, from wings to the whole bird.
I like to prepare and marinate my chicken this way for barbecues, and the burnt
tinges taste really good.*

Serves 4

4 chicken breast fillets, skinned

2 teaspoons paprika

2–3 tablespoons cooking oil

juice of 1 lemon

1 tablespoon soy sauce

salad and baked potatoes, rice or noodles, to serve

1 Cut the chicken breasts into strips about the thickness of your little finger. Dust with the paprika so that they are well coated in an even layer.

2 Heat the oil in a frying-pan. Add the chicken strips and stir-fry over a high heat for about 4–5 minutes.

3 Add the lemon juice and soy sauce and quickly boil until it reduces slightly and coats the chicken in a sticky glaze. It is now ready to serve with a salad and baked potato, rice, noodles or whatever you fancy!

Extra Rhodes . . .

- *Make this dish using chicken quarters. Dust them with the paprika and then roll them in the lemon juice and soy sauce mixture. Place in a roasting tray and cook in a pre-heated oven at 220°C/425°F/gas 7 for 25–30 minutes. Pour over the remaining soy mixture and serve.*
- *You can also fry the paprika-dusted quarters in a little oil on top of the stove, to guarantee a good, rich, golden red colour, before finishing them off in a pre-heated oven at the above temperature for a further 20–25 minutes. Then remove, drain away the excess oil and add the lemon juice and soy. Simmer, basting now and then, until well glazed.*
- *Whole chickens can be dusted with paprika before roasting and finished with the soy and lemon too. A 1.5 kg (3 lb) chicken will take about 1 hour at 200°C/400°F/gas 6.*
- *Soured cream goes very well as a dip for this dish.*

SIMPLE MEAT with speedy sauces and gravies

All meat dishes can be kept simple, whether they are braised, stewed, pan-fried or grilled. The secret of good results is good seasoning and, of course, good cooking! Braised and stewed recipes really look after themselves, while gentle cooking gives tender and tasty results, but with pan-frying and grilling, there are a few simple rules which need be followed to help give good results.

Pan-frying and grilling are ideal for so many different cuts and types of meat and poultry – chicken, pork, liver, lamb and steaks – and a sauce can lift a simple meal to new heights; it obviously makes the dish a lot richer and, often, a lot tastier too. So here are just a few tips on pan-frying and grilling, with a few short-cut sauces to follow that will all go with the meat of your choice.

pan-frying a steak

1 The first thing to do is to heat the frying-pan until it is really hot. It is important to make sure that the meat seals and starts to fry as soon as it hits the pan, otherwise it will poach. Meanwhile, season the steak with salt and freshly ground black pepper.

2 Once the steak is frying in the hot pan, it is up to you how long you leave it, depending on whether you like it rare, medium or well done.

3 While the steak is cooking, some of the juices will start to caramelize in the pan, and this is one flavour that just can't be ignored. If you are making Red Wine Sauce (opposite) to go with it, add the wine to the pan once the steak has been removed and scrape up all the caramelized juices, then finish as for the recipe. If you are not making a sauce, simply add a knob of butter to the pan to bind all those flavours and then pour it over your steak.

grilling meats

Grilling has to be the easiest method of cooking meat. The most important point to remember is to pre-heat the grill to high before you start cooking. This will make sure that the meat is sealed quickly, keeping in all its natural juices.

Extra Rhodes . . .

Here are a few options for pan-fried or grilled meats:

- *Rub the meat with a cut garlic clove before seasoning and cooking.*
- *Brush the meat with a little mustard before cooking.*
- *Sprinkle the meat with a little Worcestershire sauce before or after cooking.*
- *Add a squeeze of lemon juice to the meat after cooking.*

red or white wine sauce

I have discovered that a packet of Crosse & Blackwell Bonne Cuisine Madeira Wine Gravy or White Wine Gravy mix (see p.9) makes an ideal quick base for a well-flavoured gravy or sauce to which you can add the flavour of your choice. Add a little extra water if you prefer a slightly looser texture. Here is the basic recipe and a few more ideas to make with it.

Serves 4
300 ml (10 fl oz) red or white wine
salt and freshly ground black pepper

Optional extras:
½ onion, sliced
1 bay leaf
a few black peppercorns, lightly crushed
300 ml (10 fl oz) instant Madeira or
    White Wine Gravy (see p.9)

Put the wine and the optional extras, if using, into a pan and boil until reduced by three-quarters. Stir in the instant gravy and simmer for a few minutes before straining out all the 'extras'. Season with salt and pepper.

Extra Rhodes . . .

- *Flavour and garnish either sauce with some cooked shallot, onion, leek or sliced mushrooms.*
- *Add chopped tomatoes or herbs to the finished sauce.*
- *Add double cream to go with chicken or pork.*

chasseur sauce

This sauce is classically made with a white wine base, but red wine also works very well. It is ideal to eat with chicken or steaks.

Serves 4

1 large onion, finely chopped

225 g (8 oz) button mushrooms, sliced

300 ml (10 fl oz) white or red wine

300 ml (10 fl oz) instant Madeira or White Wine Gravy (see p.9)

2–3 tomatoes, peeled, seeded and diced

OR 2 tablespoons canned chopped tomatoes

1 teaspoon chopped fresh tarragon

salt and freshly ground black pepper

Add the onion and the mushrooms to the wine and boil until reduced by three-quarters. Add the instant gravy and simmer for a few minutes. Finish with the tomatoes, chopped tarragon and some seasoning.

sauce au poivre

This sauce is classically served with steak but would also eat well with pork chops or chicken.

Serves 4

1 onion, finely chopped

1–2 teaspoons green peppercorns in brine, drained and lightly pressed

a knob of butter

a splash of brandy

300 ml (10 fl oz) white wine

150 ml (5 fl oz) instant Madeira or White Wine Gravy (see p.9)

150 ml (5 fl oz) double cream

Cook the chopped onion and peppercorns in the butter for 1–2 minutes. Add the brandy and boil until almost dry (or flambé if you prefer). Add the wine and boil until reduced by three-quarters. Add the instant gravy and simmer for 5–6 minutes. Add the cream and return to a simmer. Cook for a further 5–6 minutes, which will allow the sauce to thicken and the pepper flavour to spread throughout.

quick onion gravy

This is one of my favourites which brings a whole new life to sausages, burgers and liver, and eats brilliantly poured into cooked Yorkshire puddings or with the Pork Meatloaf (p.72). If the onions are allowed to tinge on the edges they will give the sauce a bitter, sweet, even richer flavour and less of the instant Madeira or white wine sauce will give you a thicker 'onion relish' type of sauce.

Serves 4
4 large onions, finely chopped or sliced
a knob of butter

2 teaspoons demerara sugar
150–300 ml (5–10 fl oz) instant Madeira or White
    Wine Gravy (see p.9)
salt and freshly ground black pepper

Fry the onions in the butter until golden brown and almost burnt. Add the sugar and continue to cook for a few minutes until it begins to caramelize. Pour in the instant sauce and cook for 6–8 minutes. Season with salt and pepper and serve.

pork meatloaf

The pork for this recipe can be bought already minced, or ask a butcher to mince some pork belly for you, leaving in a reasonable fat content to give the loaf a good, succulent finish.

Serves 4–6
2 onions, chopped
1 garlic clove, crushed
15 g (½ oz) butter
675 g (1½ lb) minced pork
1 egg
2 slices white bread, crusts removed, made into crumbs
salt and freshly ground black pepper

1 Pre-heat the oven to 220°C/425°F/gas 7. Cook the onions and garlic in the butter in a pan for a few minutes until softened without colour. Allow to cool.

2 Mix the pork with the onions, egg, breadcrumbs and seasoning, so that you almost start to break up the texture of the meat.

3 Pack the mixture into a buttered 900 g (2 lb) loaf tin and cook in the oven for 35–40 minutes. Then just simply turn out, cut into thick slices and serve.

- *If you don't have a 900 g (2 lb) loaf tin, mould the mixture into a 'bloomer' shape on a sheet of buttered foil. Fold the long edges over the top and twist the ends to seal and give a firm shape. Heat a roasting tin on top of the stove with a drop or two of oil. Add the foil-wrapped loaf and cook for 2–3 minutes on each side. Transfer to the oven and cook for 35–40 minutes. Unwrap, slice and serve.*
- *You can put the bloomer loaf straight into the oven without sealing it first, but you need to add 8–10 minutes to the cooking time.*
- *Add some chopped fresh sage or thyme to the mixture for a herby finish.*
- *Add a few drops of Worcestershire sauce, mustard or horseradish sauce.*
- *Add some cooked chopped red peppers, mushrooms, chillies and basil.*
- *Shape the mixture into burger-shaped patties, grill or bake and serve in a bun or with chips, topped with Stilton or Cheddar rarebit (see p.32).*
- *Shape into meatballs and serve in a tomato sauce, onion gravy or a stew.*
- *For the ultimate finish, serve the loaf with mashed potatoes and onion gravy (see p.71).*

lancashire hot pot

You can't cut down the cooking time with stews but you can make a complete meal in one pot which simply looks after itself. Carrots give a light sweetness to this dish.

Serves 4

8 large lamb chops, trimmed of excess fat

4 lambs' kidneys, quartered and the cores snipped out with scissors

cooking oil

4–5 medium baking potatoes, peeled and sliced

2 large onions, sliced

4 carrots, peeled and cut into 5 mm (¼ in) slices

600 ml (1 pint) lamb, chicken or beef stock

a knob of butter, melted

salt and freshly ground black pepper

1 Pre-heat the oven to 180°C/350°F/gas 4. Season the chops and kidneys and fry in a little oil for a few minutes until lightly browned.

2 Lay half the sliced potatoes, onions and carrots in the base of a deep ovenproof casserole dish. Season with salt and pepper. Sit the lamb chops and kidneys on top of the vegetables and then top with the remaining sliced onions, carrots and potatoes.

3 Pour in the stock, cover and cook in the oven for 2 hours.

4 Uncover and brush the potatoes with butter. Increase the oven temperature to 220°C/425°F/gas 7. Cook for a further 30–40 minutes.

Extra Rhodes . . .

- *Use diced lamb in place of lamb chops and cook for just 1½ hours.*
- *Celery also cooks very well in the hot pot.*
- *Cook the hot pot in a pressure cooker for 30 minutes.*

beef and mushroom stew

This stew really does look after itself. The beef is simmered slowly to produce the most delicious stock which gives you a really glossy, well-flavoured sauce.

Serves 4–6
900 g (2 lb) stewing steak, cut into 3.5 cm (1½ in) cubes

cooking oil

3 onions, sliced

1 garlic clove, crushed

2 glasses red wine (about 250 ml/8 fl oz)

1.2 litres (2 pints) water

450 g (1 lb) button mushrooms, wiped

1 packet instant Madeira or White Wine Gravy (see p.9)

salt and freshly ground black pepper

1 Heat a large frying-pan with a little oil. Add half the steak and fry for a few minutes, turning now and then, to seal. Repeat with the rest.

2 Place the onions, garlic and red wine in a large pan and boil until reduced by half. Add the sautéed steak and water, bring up to a simmer, cover and cook for 1 hour. Add the mushrooms and cook for 30–40 minutes.

3 When the beef is tender, mix the gravy powder with a little water until smooth. Stir in and simmer for 5 minutes. If the sauce is thin, boil and reduce to a good consistency. Season to taste and serve.

Extra Rhodes . . .

- *Add some sliced carrots and celery to the stew with the mushrooms.*
- *Some fresh thyme, a bay leaf or orange peel will help to flavour the stew.*
- *A splash of Worcestershire sauce will liven up all the other flavours.*
- *Cook the stew in a pressure cooker for 50 minutes.*

caramelized pork fillets OR CHOPS

The caramelized coating on the pork is created by sprinkling it with sugar before pan-frying. The vinegar and ketchup give you a very quick sweet and sour finish.

Serves 4

675 g (1½ lb) pork fillet, cut into 4 even-sized pieces, OR 4 pork chops

2 teaspoons granulated sugar

1 tablespoon groundnut oil

2 tablespoons malt vinegar

2 tablespoons tomato ketchup

4 tablespoons water

salt and freshly ground black pepper

1 Pre-heat the oven to 200°C/400°F/gas 6. Season the pork with salt and pepper and then sprinkle on both sides with the sugar.

2 Place a small roasting tin or an ovenproof frying-pan over a high heat. Add the oil and the pork to the pan and cook for about 5 minutes, turning now and then, until dark golden all over.

3 Transfer the meat and the pan to the oven. Cook the pork fillet for about 6–8 minutes and the chops for about 12–15 minutes.

4 Remove the pan from the oven and place over a high heat once more. Remove the meat and add the vinegar to the pan – this will boil and reduce very quickly. Add the tomato ketchup and water and stir. It is now ready to pour over the pork and serve.

Extra Rhodes . . .

- *Add a splash of Tabasco sauce and Worcestershire sauce to the pan with the tomato ketchup to spice up the sauce.*
- *This dish also works very well with chicken breasts or leg portions.*

corned beef hash

This is the quickest corned beef hash recipe ever, and still as tasty! With just a can of corned beef, a knob of butter, an onion and some left-over cooked potatoes you can make a complete meal in a matter of minutes.

Serves 4	200 g (7 oz) corned beef, cut into rough 1 cm (½ in) dice
as a	cooking oil
snack or	15 g (½ oz) butter
2 as a	1 large onion, sliced
main	450 g (1 lb) mashed potatoes OR boiled or roasted potatoes, cut into rough
meal	1 cm (½ in) dice
	salt and freshly ground black pepper

1 Heat a 20–25 cm (8–10 in) frying-pan with a trickle of cooking oil. Add the butter and the onion and cook over a medium–high heat for a few minutes until soft and golden brown.

2 Add the corned beef and continue to fry and turn the meat for 3–4 minutes, until heated through.

3 Add the potatoes and stir to mix well with the beef and onions. Season with salt and pepper and pat down into a cake. Fry without stirring for 5–6 minutes, until golden brown underneath.

4 Turn the hash on to a board or plate and slide it back into the pan to brown on the other side. It is now ready to serve.

Extra Rhodes . . .

- *I love this dish with a fried egg on top, and a splash of Worcestershire sauce.*
- *Once the hash has been browned on one side, simply finish under the grill.*
- *Cook some garlic, mushrooms or sweet peppers with the onions.*
- *Add some chopped chillies and a dash of Tabasco for a fiery finish.*

honey roast pork WITH CRISPY CRACKLING

Crispy crackling is a real favourite of mine. To guarantee the best results, I tend to remove the skin from the joint and cook it separately, and coat the joint itself with honey for a sweet, glazed finish. The cut of pork loin that I'm using for this recipe is the eye of the meat from a row of pork chops. Ask your butcher to prepare the joint for you as it is not one easily available in supermarkets. The bones can be roasted with the joint to help flavour the gravy.

Serves 4–6

900 g–1.5 kg (2–3 lb) loin of pork, boned, skinned and tied, and the skin
    reserved for crackling

cooking oil

2 onions, cut into 1 cm (½ in) thick circles

3–4 tablespoons clear honey

150 ml (5 fl oz) instant White Wine Gravy (see p.9) or gravy mix of your choice

salt and freshly ground black pepper

1 Pre-heat the oven to 200°C/400°F/gas 6. Season the pork well with salt and pepper. Heat a little oil in a heavy-based frying-pan, add the pork, fat-side down first, and colour over a high heat. Then turn the meat over and brown on the other side.

2 For the crackling, make long, shallow cuts across the skin just down to the fat, about 1 cm (½ in) apart. Sprinkle liberally with salt and place in a small roasting tin, skin-side up. Place the onion slices in another small roasting tin and sit the pork on top.

3 Roast the crackling for about 50 minutes until the fat has melted and the skin is crisp, then remove and set aside. Roast the pork for 45 minutes.

4 Spoon the honey over the pork and return it to the oven for 10–15 minutes, basting now and then with the caramelized cooking juices.

5 Lift the pork and onions on to a plate and keep warm. Pour away the excess fat from the residue in the tin. Add the instant gravy, simmer for 3–5 minutes on top of the stove, then strain into a jug.

6 To serve, carve the pork into slices on plates and place a small pile of onions beside the pork. Top with a piece of crackling and the gravy.

Extra Rhodes . . .

- *Fresh cabbage and mashed potatoes go very well with this dish.*
- *Brush the joint of pork with Dijon or English mustard instead of honey for a spicier finish.*
- *This honey glaze also works very well with roast lamb or bacon.*
- *Serve this honey roast pork with a bowl of leek risotto (see p. 49).*

bacon in the pot

Bacon collar can be bought rolled, skinned, tied and ready to cook. The beauty of boiling it is that it then creates its own stock in which to cook the vegetables and potatoes. I always soak bacon joints in cold water for 24 hours before cooking, but a lot of butchers do also sell it pre-soaked.

Serves 4–6 1 × 900 g–1.5 kg (2–3 lb) cut of rolled bacon collar, pre-soaked

900 g (2 lb) prepared mixed vegetables (I like to use peeled button onions, thickly sliced carrots, celery and leeks, chunks of swede, turnip, new potatoes and peas)

a knob of butter

freshly ground black pepper

1 Cover the bacon with water in a large pan and bring to a simmer, skimming off any impurities as they rise to the surface. Cover with a lid and simmer for 1–1¼ hours.

2 It's now time to add the vegetables. Continue to cook for 20–25 minutes until all the vegetables are cooked (add any frozen peas or green vegetables for the last few minutes of cooking).

3 Remove the bacon from the pot and slice. Sit the bacon in large bowls or plates. Add a knob of butter to the cooking liquor and vegetables and season with a twist of pepper. Now simply divide the potatoes and vegetables between the bowls or plates and spoon over some of the cooking liquor.

Extra Rhodes . . .

- *Add a bay leaf and a few black peppercorns to the bacon while it's cooking.*
- *For extra flavour and colour, finish with some chopped fresh parsley.*
- *Half-cover the joint with vegetable or chicken stock and cook in a pressure cooker for 15 minutes per 450 g (1 lb).*

roast leg of lamb WITH BOULANGÈRE POTATOES

This recipe (illustrated on p. 42–43) is so easy to make – you don't even need a roasting tin for the lamb! All you need to do is roast the lamb on an open shelf in the oven with the potatoes sitting on the shelf below. They will collect and absorb all the flavours and juices released from the meat as it cooks, giving them a fuller finished taste and texture.

Serves 4–6

1 x 1.5 kg (3–3 ½ lb) leg of lamb
2 garlic cloves, thinly sliced
a sprig of fresh rosemary
1 tablespoon cooking oil
salt and freshly ground black pepper

For the boulangère potatoes:
900 g (2 lb) potatoes, peeled and thickly sliced
3 onions, sliced
300 ml (10 fl oz) chicken or vegetable stock
salt and freshly ground black pepper

1 Pre-heat the oven to 220°C/425°F/gas 7. Layer the potatoes, onions and some seasoning in a roasting tin or shallow ovenproof dish large enough to sit neatly underneath the leg of lamb. Finish the top layer by overlapping the slices of potato for a neater finish. Pour over the stock and set to one side.

2 Make small, deep incisions all over the surface of the lamb and insert the slices of garlic and small sprigs of rosemary. Season.

3 Heat the oil in a large frying-pan, add the lamb and cook for a few minutes, turning now and then, until coloured to a golden brown.

4 Place the potatoes into the oven and sit the lamb on the rack above. Cook for between 1 hour 10 minutes to 1 hour 20 minutes for a medium–rare finish. Leave the lamb to rest for 10–15 minutes and then carve and serve with the boulangère potatoes.

Extra Rhodes . . .

- *Serve the lamb with perhaps a Red Wine Sauce (see p.69).*
- *I like to serve this dish with roasted parsnips and buttered cabbage.*
- *The leg of lamb can be trickled with honey for a sweet glaze 10 minutes before the end of cooking.*
- *Layer up some leeks with the potatoes before cooking.*
- *Add some garlic and rosemary to the potatoes and leave the lamb plain.*

uddings and cakes

soufflés (p.106)

*t*he one dessert we've probably all been afraid or are afraid of making is soufflé. If you're having a dinner party, you've probably played it safe and gone for a pudding that sits in the fridge, or made a delicious chocolate fudge cake or fruit flan. Soufflés sound like hard work: you have to make a soufflé base before you can even think about the next step, and then worry about whether the soufflé will rise or not. With this recipe you can leave those worries behind. My Lemon Soufflé (p.106) lifts a simple can of custard to new heights!

I also offer you recipes for 'steamed' sponges cooked in minutes in a microwave (p.94), Melted Chocolate Brownies from Mars® bars (p.98) and Home-made Lemonade in a liquidizer (p.118)! And one I just have to tell you about is a pudding that's featured in *Open Rhodes Around Britain*. I'm convinced it will become as popular as Bread and Butter Pudding and it's called Alternative Jaffa Cake Pudding (p.116). I've basically taken the idea from the famous biscuit: a good orange jelly sandwiched between a sponge base and a chocolate topping. The recipe in this book is much quicker and easier to make than the one in *Open Rhodes* and still tastes sensational – the different textures and flavours all complement each other. It can also be made well in advance and will last in your fridge for a good few days, so there's no excuse – it has to be tried!

You're now in the last chapter and I hope you've managed to try some of the recipes and found your cooking has accelerated to new levels. You'll find some of the recipes are in the inside lane, some in the middle lane and the rest in the fast lane. As with any Grand Prix, the one thing I do hope is that they all have the right formula to reach the chequered flag!

lemon, lime or orange posset

This pudding can be any one of these three flavours, and could even be a combination of lemon and lime, or orange and lemon. The reaction of the sugar and the acidic juices of the fruits with the cream is amazing! It's a very popular dessert that can be made at quite short notice.

Serves 6

900 ml (1½ pints) double cream
250 g (9 oz) caster sugar
juice of 3 lemons
a little single cream, to serve

1 Put the cream, sugar and lemon juice into a pan. Bring to the boil and boil for 3 minutes.

2 Leave the mixture to cool slightly and then pour into 6 glasses and refrigerate for at least 1–2 hours.

3 Before serving, pour 5 mm (¼ in) of single cream on to the top of each one, to balance the richness.

Extra Rhodes . . .

- *Use the juice of 4 limes instead of lemon juice for a lime posset.*
- *For an orange posset, finely grate the zest from 1 orange. Squeeze the juice from 3 oranges and boil until reduced by half before adding the cream and the sugar. For a deeper flavour, 1–2 tablespoons of marmalade can be added to the mix once cooked.*
- *For a chocolate orange pudding, serve the orange posset with a chocolate sauce made by boiling 50–75 ml (2–3 fl oz) of cream, then stirring in 50 g (2 oz) of melted plain chocolate.*

toffee cream pots

This 'toffee' always amazes me. Unopened and refrigerated it keeps almost indefinitely. This recipe lightens the flavour of the toffee and – together with one of the additions listed below – makes it into a really easy, tasty pudding.

Serves 4

1 x 200 g (7 oz) can sweetened condensed milk

½ x 425 g (15 oz) carton OR can ready-made custard

150 ml (5 fl oz) double cream

1 Place the unopened can of condensed milk in a pan and cover with plenty of cold water. Bring to the boil and simmer for 3 hours. Leave to cool in the pan. Spoon the 'toffee' out of the can into a bowl and whisk in the custard.

2 Whip the cream until it just begins to thicken but doesn't quite form peaks. Gently fold into the toffee custard.

3 Spoon the mixture into 4 ramekins or glasses (or even tea cups, would be ideal) and chill in the fridge for about 1 hour until firm.

Extra Rhodes...

- *Cover the top of each pot with some sliced bananas, toasted nibbed almonds and a little icing sugar.*
- *For a chocolate topping, melt 100 g (4 oz) of good-quality plain chocolate with 25 g (1 oz) of butter. Pour on top of each pot and set in the fridge.*
- *For a trifle finish, sit some sponge fingers in the bottom of each pot, soak with rum and then cover with the toffee mix.*
- *Pipe some whipped cream on top of each pot, drizzle with a little maple syrup and decorate with a few toasted flaked almonds.*
- *Add some rum-soaked raisins or currants to the mixture before setting.*

ICE-CREAMS and sauces

Classic vanilla ice-cream means lots of cream, eggs and fresh vanilla. Here's a ready-made base for ice-cream — nothing more simple than a can of custard to which just about any flavour can be added. This method is one that doesn't require an ice-cream machine, but if you do have one then simply don't whip the cream before churning. A couple of quick sauce ideas follow.

basic custard ice-cream

Serves 4
150 ml (5 fl oz) double cream

425 g (15 oz) carton OR can ready-made custard
a dash or two of vanilla essence

1 Whip the cream until it forms soft peaks — in other words the tips of the peaks flop over instead of standing upright.

2 Fold the cream into the custard, with the vanilla essence, until evenly mixed. Spoon into a plastic container, cover and freeze, stirring from time to time, until firm.

Extra Rhodes . . .

Here are some extra flavours that can be added to the basic ice-cream for the flavour of your choice:

- *Cut 100–175 g (4–6 oz) of Turkish delight into small pieces and stir in with a few drops of rose water, if you wish.*

- *Mash 225 g (8 oz) of ripe bananas with a few drops of lemon juice and stir into the ice-cream mix.*
- *Add some finely chopped left-over Christmas pudding for a rich festive treat.*
- *Add 225 g (8 oz) of clear honey and whisky to taste.*
- *Stir in 225 g (8 oz) of marmalade.*
- *Stir in 175 g (6 oz) of melted plain, milk or white chocolate.*
- *Add 50 g (2 oz) each of chopped toasted hazelnuts and almonds and 100 g (4 oz) of raisins to a chocolate ice-cream mix for a 'fruit and nut' finish.*
- *Add some rum or Cointreau to taste to a chocolate ice-cream.*
- *Add 2–3 tablespoons of good marmalade to a chocolate ice-cream.*

soft fruit ice-creams

Serves 4

225 g (8 oz) soft fruits such as strawberries
  or raspberries

2 tablespoons icing sugar (or more to taste)
200 ml (7 fl oz) tub crème fraîche

Mash the fruits with the icing sugar until smooth. Press through a sieve or leave grainy. Mix with the crème fraîche, spoon into a bowl and freeze, stirring occasionally, until firm.

lemon curd ice-cream

Serves 4

300–350 g (11–12 oz) jar lemon curd

200 ml (7 fl oz) tub crème fraîche
4 large tablespoons natural yoghurt

Simply mix all the ingredients together and spoon into a bowl. Place the bowl in the freezer and stir from time to time, until the mixture is firm.

ultimate chocolate sauce

Serves 4

225 g (8 oz) good-quality plain chocolate

250 ml (8 fl oz) double cream
25 g (1 oz) unsalted butter

Melt the chocolate with the cream in a bowl set over a pan of simmering water. Stir in the butter until melted, remove from the heat and serve.

mars® bar sauce

Serves 4

1 x 65 g (2½ oz) Mars® bar, sliced

a few tablespoons single cream (optional)

Simply put the sliced Mars® bar into a bowl set over a pan of simmering water and leave until it has melted into a milky, chocolate toffee sauce. To make it softer and less strong, stir in the single cream.

microwave 'steamed' puddings

I've pinched this recipe from my mother. It's such a quick pudding to make and cooks in minutes. Simply serve with one of the custard sauces on p.96.

Serves 4–6
100 g (4 oz) self-raising flour
100 g (4 oz) butter, softened
100 g (4 oz) caster sugar
2 medium eggs

1 Lightly butter and flour a 900 ml–1.2 litre (1½–2 pint) pudding basin. Put all the ingredients into a food processor and blitz until smooth. If necessary, add a few drops of milk to give a soft consistency.

2 Sit the flavour of your choice (see below) in the base of the basin and spoon the sponge mixture on top. Cover with clingfilm and pierce it with a knife.

3 For a 500-watt microwave, cook on high for 4½–5 minutes or until a skewer pushed into the centre of the sponge comes out clean. For every 100 watts above this, take about 15 seconds off the cooking time (i.e. 3½–4 minutes in a 1000-watt microwave). Now simply turn it out and enjoy!

Extra Rhodes . . .

- *Spoon 2–3 tablespoons of golden syrup (my favourite!), jam, marmalade, fruit curd, stewed apples or rhubarb into the base of the basin.*
- *If you are making a golden syrup, lemon curd or marmalade pudding, add 1 or 2 tablespoons of the flavouring to the pudding mix itself for extra taste.*
- *Add some finely grated lemon or orange zest to the pudding mix itself.*
- *For a rich chocolate pudding, replace 25 g (1 oz) of the flour with cocoa powder and stir 100–225 g (4–8 oz) of grated plain chocolate into the mix.*

custard sauces

Ready-made custard can be turned into so many different sauces. Here are a few ideas to be working on. As well as being the perfect accompaniment to steamed puddings, they also go very well served with the sweet soufflés on p.106 and the Home-made Doughnuts (see p.104).

To 1 x 425 g (15 oz) carton or can of ready-made custard add one of the following:

■ 4 tablespoons lemon curd and 2 tablespoons lemon juice
■ 4 tablespoons orange marmalade and 4 tablespoons orange juice
  (and perhaps a touch of Grand Marnier too!)
■ 6 tablespoons golden syrup
■ 6 tablespoons black treacle
■ 4 tablespoons clear honey
■ 4 tablespoons maple syrup
■ 2–3 teaspoons Camp coffee essence OR 1 tablespoon instant coffee granules,
  dissolved in 1 teaspoon of boiling water
■ dark rum or Cointreau to taste
■ 4–5 tablespoons single or double cream for a richer, creamier consistency

Simply warm the ready-made custard in a pan with the flavouring of your choice and it's ready to serve.

banana bread cake

I had to include this recipe from Rhodes Around Britain. *In that recipe, the cake is topped with 50 g (2 oz) of pecan nuts before it is baked, so if you want to include these, please do. Hazelnuts or walnuts could also be used.*

Makes	3 large ripe bananas (over-ripe are even better)
1 x 900 g	225 g (8 oz) self-raising flour
(2 lb)	175 g (6 oz) caster sugar
loaf	100 g (4 oz) unsalted butter
	2 eggs
	2 tablespoons golden syrup
	a pinch of salt

1 Pre-heat the oven to 150°C/300°F/gas 2. Peel the bananas, slice into a bowl and mash with a fork until smooth. Beat in all the remaining ingredients until completely combined. This could also be done in a food mixer or food processor.

2 Spoon the mixture into a greased 900 g (2 lb) loaf tin and bake for 1¼ hours until risen and firm to touch. Leave to rest for 10–15 minutes before turning out of the tin. The cake is now ready and can be served as a warm pudding or just left to cool.

Extra Rhodes . . .

- *For a richer 'toffee' flavour, replace the golden syrup with black treacle.*
- *Melt some chocolate and pour over the top for a banana and chocolate cake.*
- *For the ultimate finish, serve with Vanilla Ice-cream and the Ultimate Chocolate Sauce (p. 93).*

melted chocolate brownies

As you will see, this is a very quick and easy recipe. These brownies eat very well as a pudding with vanilla ice-cream or pouring cream.

Makes	100 g (4 oz) butter
about	3 × 65 g (2½ oz) Mars® bars
9–12	75 g (3 oz) rice crispies or cornflakes
brownies	100 g (4 oz) plain chocolate

1 Lightly grease a 15 cm (6 in) shallow square tin with butter. Cut the Mars® bars into thin slices and place in a large pan with 75 g (3 oz) of the butter. Leave the mixture over a low heat until melted and then beat until smooth.

2 Stir in the rice crispies or cornflakes and then spread the mixture into the prepared tin. Chill in the fridge for 1 hour or until set.

3 To finish, place the chocolate and the rest of the butter into a small bowl and rest it over a pan of simmering water until melted. Spread on top of the set brownies and return to the fridge until set. Cut into squares or bars to serve.

Extra Rhodes . . .

- *Add grated orange zest or a splash of dark rum to the Mars® bar slices while they're melting.*
- *Stir a few raisins or currants into the mixture with the rice crispies.*
- *To give a shiny glaze, place the brownies under a hot grill for a few seconds just before serving.*

chocolate mousse

This recipe gives you a good, rich chocolate mousse with a light finish. It's best made with plain chocolate for maximum taste, but milk or white chocolate can also be used. If you prefer not to use raw egg, follow the alternative opposite which uses custard instead.

Serves 4

225 g (8 oz) good-quality plain chocolate

2 egg yolks

50 g (2 oz) caster sugar

300 ml (10 fl oz) double cream

pouring cream or orange segments, to decorate

1 Break the chocolate into a medium-sized bowl and rest it over a pan of simmering water, making sure that the bowl does not touch the water. Leave until melted.

2 Whisk the yolks and sugar together in another bowl until light and fluffy.

3 Whip the cream into soft peaks – the tips of the peaks should flip over rather than stand upright.

4 Carefully stir the melted chocolate into the egg yolk mix, then gently fold in the whipped cream.

5 Pour the mixture into 4 glasses and chill in the fridge for 2–3 hours, until set. Decorate with a little pouring cream or orange segments.

Extra Rhodes...

- *For a lighter finish, fold in the lightly whisked egg whites after the cream.*
- *For an even quicker short-cut recipe, replace the egg yolks and sugar with half a 425 g (15 oz) carton or can of ready-made custard. Stir in the melted chocolate, fold in the whipped cream and chill in the glasses until set.*
- *Add a little dark rum or Cointreau with the melted chocolate.*
- *Whisk a little finely grated orange zest into the egg yolk mixture.*
- *Lightly fold in a few finely chopped walnuts or toasted hazelnuts.*
- *Place some broken sponge fingers into the bottom of the glasses and soak in rum or Cointreau before pouring in the chocolate mousse.*

marmalade and almond cake

During cooking the sponge rises and then sinks down in the middle as it cools, so don't worry or feel that it has failed, because it hasn't, and it eats beautifully.

Makes
1 x 900 g
(2 lb)
loaf

3 eggs
100 g (4 oz) ground almonds
50 g (2 oz) caster sugar
a good pinch of baking powder
175 g (6 oz) fine or medium-cut orange marmalade

1 Pre-heat the oven to 180°C/350°F/gas 4. Lightly grease a 900 g (2 lb) loaf tin with butter and line with greaseproof paper.

2 Crack the eggs into a large mixing bowl and whisk vigorously until the mixture is thick and mousse-like, and leaves a visible trail over the surface (known as the 'ribbon stage').

3 Mix the almonds with the sugar and baking powder. Gently fold into the eggs, with the marmalade, until well mixed.

4 The mix can now be poured into the prepared tin and baked for about 30 minutes. To check if it is cooked, pierce with a skewer or knife. When it comes out clean, the cake is cooked. Now it's ready to enjoy as a pudding with clotted cream or simply as a slice of cake.

Extra Rhodes . . .

- *Other flavoured marmalades can also be used – ginger, lemon or lime all work equally well.*
- *Top each slice with fresh orange segments and glaze with icing sugar.*

home-made doughnuts

These are so easy to make and even better to eat. The fillings are up to you and they will eat really well as a bun or as a full pudding, served with ice-cream, clotted or pouring cream, plain custard or a custard sauce (see p.96).

**Makes 4
doughnuts**

8 teaspoons strawberry jam

8 thick slices white bread, buttered

25 g (1 oz) caster sugar

100 g (4 oz) self-raising flour

150 ml (5 fl oz) strong dry cider

cooking oil, for deep-frying

1 Spoon the jam into the centre of the buttered side of 4 slices of the bread. Sit the other slices of bread on top, butter–side down. Press and seal the two slices together around the jam.

2 You can now cut a disc from the bread using a cup or a 7.5 cm (3 in) plain pastry cutter. These can be made in advance and chilled until needed.

3 For the batter, mix the sugar and flour together. Whisk in the cider until you have a thick batter. Heat a deep-fat fryer or a pan of oil to 180°C/350°F (see p.8).

4 Dip the sandwiches in the batter and fry in the hot oil for a few minutes until golden and crispy on one side. They now need to be turned over with a slotted spoon and cooked for a few more minutes. Remove them from the oil and drain on kitchen paper. Dust with caster sugar and serve.

Extra Rhodes...

- Use any flavoured jam as the filling – raspberry, blackcurrant or whatever you prefer.
- Fill the doughnuts with marmalade (orange, lemon or lime) or lemon curd.
- Fill them with mincemeat for 'mince pie' doughnuts.
- Fill with chunky apple sauce, cooked rhubarb or canned fruits such as cherries or apricots.
- For savoury doughnuts, replace the cider with lager and omit the sugar from the batter. Fill with sausagemeat as a great alternative to sausage rolls.

lemon soufflé

How many times do we make soufflés at home? Not enough, I say! Soufflés are a wonderful dessert and, when you see how easy this recipe is (illustrated on p.86–87), I'm sure they'll become a firm family favourite. The base for the recipe is simply canned custard. All you have to do is to add the flavour of your choice and some whisked egg whites. You can also use 6 x 7.5 cm (3 in) ordinary ramekins instead of the soufflé ones.

Makes	a knob of butter
4 x 10 cm	50 g (2 oz) caster sugar, plus extra for coating the ramekins
(4 in)	4 medium egg whites
soufflé	8 tablespoons ready-made custard
ramekins	finely grated zest and juice of 2 small lemons
	2 egg yolks (optional, for a richer taste)
	icing sugar, for dusting

1 Pre-heat the oven to 220°C/425°F/gas 7. Place a baking sheet in the oven to heat, too. Lightly grease the inside of the ramekins with butter and then coat with a layer of caster sugar, making sure that it comes right up to the rims.

2 Whisk the egg whites and sugar until the mixture forms soft peaks – the tips of the peaks should flip over, not stand upright.

3 Mix the custard with the lemon zest, lemon juice and egg yolks, if using. Fold in one-quarter of the egg whites and then carefully fold in the rest.

4 Spoon the mixture into the ramekins, filling to just below the rim, and bake in the oven for 9–10 minutes for the smaller ones, 10–12 minutes for the larger ones. They can now be lightly dusted with icing sugar through a tea strainer, to finish.

Extra Rhodes . . .

- *For a lemon sauce to serve with the lemon soufflés, warm and loosen the remaining custard with a little milk or single cream and flavour with a little lemon juice. Sweeten with caster or icing sugar to taste.*
- *If you are serving a sauce with soufflés, split open the tops of them at the table and pour in the hot sauce. It will almost re-soufflé the pudding!*
- *Drop a spoonful of home-made ice-cream (see p.92) into the top of each soufflé, with or without the hot sauce.*
- *Replace the lemon zest and juice in the lemon soufflés with 5 tablespoons of lemon curd.*
- *For orange soufflés, finely grate the zest from 1 orange. Squeeze the juice from 2 oranges and boil until reduced by three-quarters. Leave to cool, then add to the basic mixture, with the zest. You could also add a splash of Grand Marnier and Cointreau to the basic mixture here.*
- *For even richer orange soufflés, add 2 teaspoons of marmalade to the bottom of each ramekin. It will create its own sauce in the bottom during cooking.*
- *For summer fruit soufflés (strawberry, raspberry or whatever) replace the lemon zest and juice with 1 tablespoon of jam per person. Cover the base of the ramekins with some fresh fruit before covering with the mixture and baking.*
- *Flavour the custard with 100 g (4 oz) melted plain or milk chocolate and a splash of rum for a wonderful rich chocolate soufflé. Serve with the Mars® Bar Sauce on p.93.*

BREAD AND BUTTER PUDDINGS and more!

For me, there really is no short cut with this pudding, but I wanted to include it because the recipe lends itself beautifully to other ideas. Here is my 'classic' way of making it, and some ideas for some similar puddings too.

classic bread and butter pudding

Serves 6–8

50 g (2 oz) unsalted butter, softened
12 medium-thick slices white bread, crusts removed
8 egg yolks
175 g (6 oz) caster sugar
a few drops of vanilla essence

300 ml (10 fl oz) milk
300 ml (10 fl oz) double cream
25 g (1 oz) sultanas
25 g (1 oz) raisins
caster sugar, to finish

1 Pre-heat the oven to 180°C/350°F/gas 4. Lightly butter a 1.75 litre (3 pint) shallow ovenproof pudding dish. Spread the bread with the rest of the butter and then cut each slice diagonally into 4 triangles.

2 Whisk the egg yolks, caster sugar and vanilla essence together in a bowl. Put the milk and the cream into a pan, bring to a simmer and then stir into the egg yolks.

3 Layer one-third of the bread in the bottom of the prepared dish. Sprinkle with half the sultanas and raisins. Repeat once more and then finish with a final layer of bread without any fruit as this tends to burn if it is on the top of the pudding.

4 The warm egg custard can now be poured over the bread and baked straight away.

5 Place the dish in a roasting tray, three-quarters filled with warm water and bake in the oven for 20–30 minutes.

6 Pre-heat your grill to medium–high. Remove the dish from the roasting tray and sprinkle liberally with caster sugar. Slide under the grill and glaze – the sugar will dissolve and caramelize. Your pudding is now ready to serve.

Extra Rhodes...

- *The pudding can be left to soak up the custard for 20–30 minutes before cooking.*
- *A gas gun can be used, with care, to glaze the top.*
- *Spread the buttered bread with marmalade, lemon curd or jam before layering, keeping the top layer clear for glazing. You could also add a little grated lemon or orange zest to the egg custard for extra flavour.*
- *Spread the bread with a little mincemeat before layering and add a splash of rum to the egg custard for a Christmas mince-pie-flavoured pudding.*
- *Sprinkle with a little grated plain, milk or white chocolate and melt under the grill before serving.*
- *Top with thin slices of peeled orange before glazing with the sugar.*
- *Top a lemon-flavoured pudding with meringue as for lemon meringue.*
- *Top a jam pudding with meringue for a special 'Queen of Puddings'.*

black forest bread and butter pudding

This is a fun pudding to try. The rich flavours of chocolate and cherries work so well together.

Serves 6–8

12 small slices buttered bread, crusts removed
4 tablespoons cherry jam
300 ml (10 fl oz) chocolate milk

300 ml (10 fl oz) double cream
3 eggs
50 g (2 oz) caster sugar
175 g (6 oz) plain chocolate, finely grated

1 Pre-heat the oven to 180°C/350°F/gas 4. Spread half the bread with the jam. Cut all the slices diagonally into 4 small triangles.

2 Layer the cherry jam slices in a buttered 1.75 litre (3 pint) shallow ovenproof pudding dish. Finish the top layer with the plain bread and butter triangles.

3 Put the chocolate milk and cream into a pan and slowly bring to the boil. Meanwhile whisk the eggs and sugar together in a bowl.

4 Stir 100 g (4 oz) of the chocolate into the hot cream and milk. Once the chocolate has melted, take off the heat and whisk into the eggs and sugar.

5 Pour the hot custard over the bread and leave to stand for 15–20 minutes.

6 Place the dish in a roasting tray, three-quarters filled with warm water and bake in the oven for 20–30 minutes. .

7 Remove from the oven and sprinkle over the remaining grated chocolate. Once it has melted it is ready to serve.

Extra Rhodes . . .

- *Place drained canned cherries or fresh stoned ones in the base of the dish for a fruitier finish.*
- *Instead of finishing with chocolate, sprinkle with caster or demerara sugar and slide under a hot grill until the sugar has dissolved and caramelized.*
- *Serve with some pouring cream.*
- *For an even richer chocolate bread and butter pudding, spread the bread with chocolate spread instead of cherry jam.*

loaf cake bread and butter pudding

I like to buy a golden syrup, ginger, lemon or orange loaf cake, spread butter on to the slices and make into a bread and butter pudding. Here's the recipe!

Serves 4–6

1 x 450 g (1 lb) loaf-style cake, cut into
   1 cm (½ in) slices
25 g (1 oz) unsalted butter, softened

200 ml (7 fl oz) milk
200 ml (7 fl oz) double cream
3 eggs
50 g (2 oz) caster sugar

1 Pre-heat the oven to 180°C/350°F/gas 4. Spread the slices of cake with the butter and then arrange, slightly overlapping, over the base of a buttered 1.75 litre (3 pint) shallow ovenproof pudding dish.

2 Bring the milk and the cream to the boil in a pan. Meanwhile whisk the eggs and sugar together in a bowl.

3 Pour the hot milk and cream on to the eggs. Strain the custard over the layered cake and set aside for 20 minutes if you wish.

4 Place the dish in a roasting tray, three-quarters filled with warm water and bake in the oven for about 20 minutes until thickened but not set.

5 Finish as for the classic bread and butter pudding or with the Extra Rhodes opposite.

griddled scones

These scones, illustrated overleaf, are not baked but pan-fried instead. Of course, the classic combination of strawberry jam and clotted cream go beautifully with these.

Makes about 10 scones

225 g (8 oz) self-raising flour plus extra for dusting

a pinch of salt

50 g (2 oz) butter, cut into small pieces, plus extra for frying

75 g (3 oz) currants or sultanas

50 g (2 oz) caster sugar

1 egg, beaten

1–2 tablespoons milk

1 Sift the flour and salt into a bowl. Rub in the butter until the mixture looks like fine breadcrumbs. This can be done in a food processor if you wish.

2 Stir in the dried fruit and sugar. Make a well in the centre and add the egg and the milk. Gradually mix everything together to make a soft dough.

3 Turn the mixture out on to a surface dusted with flour, dust the top of the dough with a little more flour and roll out to a thickness of 1 cm (½ in).

4 This can now be cut with a knife or a pastry cutter into 6 cm (2½ in) rounds. Re-knead and roll the trimmings to make about 10 scones in total.

5 Heat a frying-pan over a medium heat. Melt a knob of butter, add 3 or 4 scones and fry for 5–6 minutes on each side until golden brown. Cool on a wire rack while you cook the rest of the scones.

Extra Rhodes . . .

- *These scones can also be baked at 220°C/425°F/gas 7 for 10–12 minutes.*
- *Eat the scones hot or cold with clotted cream and fresh strawberries or raspberries.*
- *Add the finely grated zest of 1 lemon or orange to the dry ingredients.*
- *Add some chopped glacé fruits to the dry mixture with the dried fruit.*
- *Add a little peeled and diced apple to the dry ingredients with the dried fruit.*
- *Flavour the scones with a little ground cinnamon or freshly grated nutmeg.*
- *Replace 50 g (2 oz) of the flour with cocoa powder for chocolate scones.*
- *If you're making chocolate scones, drizzle with Mars® Bar Sauce (p. 93).*
- *Serve with any one of the ice-creams on p. 92–3.*

OVERLEAF

Left: Griddled Scones (p. 112)

Right: Alternative Jaffa Cake Pudding (p. 116)

alternative jaffa cake pudding

This pudding is a must, and what I mean by that is you MUST try it! It really is very good to eat and this alternative (illustrated on p.115) to the original recipe in Open Rhodes Around Britain *is much simpler and quicker, and makes enough to feed the whole family. The sponge flan case is one of those ready-made varieties found in all supermarkets.*

Serves 6–8
1 x packet orange jelly, cut into squares
375 ml (13 fl oz) orange juice
275 g (10 oz) plain chocolate, broken into pieces
350 ml (12 fl oz) double cream
1 x 25 cm (10 in) sponge flan case
pouring cream, to serve

1 Put the orange jelly into a jug and pour on 150 ml (5 fl oz) of boiling orange juice. Stir until dissolved and then stir in the rest of the orange juice. Pour it into a 23 cm (9 in) shallow, round cake tin or dish lined with clingfilm and chill until set. The finished disc of jelly needs to be about 1 cm (½ in) thick.

2 For the chocolate topping, put the chocolate and half the cream into a bowl and rest over a pan of simmering water until melted. Remove and leave to cool. Whip the rest of the cream into soft peaks – the tips of the peaks should flip over, not stand upright. Fold into the melted chocolate mix and chill for a few minutes to a spreading consistency, but do not let it set.

3 Turn the jelly out of the tin and remove the clingfilm. Now sit it in the sponge flan case and spread over the topping, making sure that the jelly is completely covered and a 'domed' top is achieved.

4 Leave to set in the fridge for at least 30 minutes before serving. The jaffa cake pudding is now ready. I like to serve it with a little more pouring cream.

Extra Rhodes . . .

- *Slide the pudding under the grill for a few seconds for a rich, shiny finish.*
- *For a richer, moister sponge, boil 150 ml (5 fl oz) of orange juice with 25 g (1 oz) of sugar until reduced by one-third. Cool and sprinkle over the sponge.*
- *Add Cointreau, Grand Marnier or orange syrup to the jelly for extra flavour.*
- *Instead of glazing the top, simply dust with cocoa powder or finely grated chocolate.*
- *For an even richer glaze, melt 225 g (8 oz) plain chocolate and 50 g (2 oz) butter in a bowl and rest over a pan of simmering water until melted. Spread all over the jaffa cake.*

home-made lemonade OR LIMEADE

This really is very quick. It's all put into a blender, passed through a sieve and that's it! Orangeade can also be made but half the quantity of water should be replaced with orange juice for a really rich flavour.

2 whole lemons or 3 limes, chopped (including the pith and peel)

4 tablespoons caster sugar

600 ml (1 pint) water

Blitz all the ingredients to a purée in a liquidizer and then push through a sieve. More sugar may be added for a sweeter finish. This can now be chilled and served on ice. A quick and very refreshing drink is born!

SWEET TARTS

Here are two recipes that, with the help of the additions and alternatives below, can become very many more.

to make a basic pastry tart case

225 g (8 oz) ready-made shortcrust or sweet shortcrust pastry

1 Lightly grease a 20–25 cm (8–10 in) loose-bottomed flan tin. Roll out the pastry on a lightly floured surface into a round slightly larger than the tin.

2 Lift the pastry over the flan tin and carefully press on to the base and up the sides, leaving the edges overhanging.

3 Run a rolling pin over the top of the tin to remove the excess pastry. Prick the base here and there with a fork and chill for 20 minutes. Pre-heat the oven to 180°C/350°F/gas 4.

4 Line the pastry case with a sheet of greaseproof paper. Cover the base with a generous layer of baking beans or rice and bake in the oven for 15–20 minutes. Remove the paper and beans. Your tart case is now ready to use.

NOTE: For absolute security of a perfect finish with no shrinking, you can cook the pastry case with the excess pastry overhanging the edge of the tin. Cook in the normal fashion and then trim away the excess pastry once it has cooked. You will now have a perfect finish around the top edge of the case.

treacle tart and other flavours

Here is a very easy tart to make, and if you buy a tart case ready-made
the recipe can be made even quicker!

Serves 6–8

1 ready-baked 20–23 cm (8–9 in) tart case
50 g (2 oz) butter
10 tablespoons golden syrup

8 slices white bread, crusts removed and made into
   crumbs
finely grated zest and juice of 1 lemon

1 Pre-heat the oven to 180°C/350°F/gas 4.
Melt the butter and syrup together in a pan.
Stir in the breadcrumbs, lemon zest and
juice. Pour the mixture into the case and
bake for 20 minutes.

2 When the treacle filling is beginning to
bubble, the tart is ready. If not, simply cook for
another 5–10 minutes. Once cooked, remove
the tart from the oven and leave to settle. It
can now be served either warm or cold.

Extra Rhodes...

- *Add a good pinch of ground ginger to the mixture for
  a spicier finish.*
- *Add the grated zest of ½ orange or 2 limes together
  with the lemon zest.*
- *Add a few tablespoons of double cream and
  1 or 2 eggs for a richer tart.*
- *For Hallowe'en, use half golden syrup half black treacle.*
- *Replace quarter of the golden syrup with marmalade
  or jam, for a fruity taste. Decorate with fresh fruit.*

gypsy tart

Looking at the list of ingredients tells you how easy and uncomplicated this recipe is. It's a childhood favourite of mine and one that becomes very moreish.

Serves 6–8

1 x ready-baked 25 cm (10 in) tart case
1 x 400 g (14 oz) can evaporated milk

350 g (12 oz) muscovado sugar
  (no other sugar will work!)
pouring cream, to serve

1 Pre-heat the oven to 200°C/400°F/gas 6. Whisk together the evaporated milk and sugar with an electric mixer for a minimum of 10–15 minutes. The mix will become coffee coloured with the consistency of whipped cream. It is important to get to this stage before going on to the next.

2 Pour the mix into the pastry case and bake for 10 minutes. Remove from the oven and leave to cool before slicing and serving with some pouring cream to finish it off.

NOTE

■ Chill the evaporated milk for at least an hour before whisking to guarantee a whisking consistency.

■ When whisking, keep the machine on maximum speed.

■ The tart is best eaten at room temperature and not refrigerated.

■ Don't be tempted to use another sugar: only muscovado sugar works for this recipe.

speedy 'sweet risotto' rice pudding

Risotto is usually a savoury dish but I thought I'd give you a new idea for a rice pudding, made with the classic arborio risotto rice. It's sensational!

Serves 4

175 g (6 oz) arborio rice

1 litre (1¾ pints) milk

75 g (3 oz) caster sugar

½ teaspoon vanilla essence

50 g (2 oz) unsalted butter

1 Pour the milk into a pan and bring up to the boil. Stir in the sugar and vanilla essence and keep hot over a low heat.

2 Melt the butter in a large pan. Stir in the rice and cook on a medium heat for a few minutes, without letting the rice colour.

3 Pour a ladle of the hot milk on to the rice and simmer gently, stirring, until the rice has absorbed all the milk.

4 Continue to cook the rice like this, adding more milk as each ladle is absorbed, for 30–40 minutes or until the rice is tender and creamy in texture.

5 That's the basic recipe made. Now choose one of the options opposite to finish.

Extra Rhodes . . .

- *I like to add some single or double cream at the end of cooking for a creamier finish.*
- *Grate some fresh nutmeg over the top for a classic finish.*
- *Omit the sugar and sweeten with some honey or golden syrup instead.*
- *Add some finely grated lemon or orange zest and juice to the risotto towards the end of cooking.*
- *Top the finished risotto with a little jam before serving. Children will love it.*
- *Stir in 225 g (8 oz) of finely grated plain, milk or white chocolate at the end.*
- *Serve the finished risotto with prepared fresh fruits such as bananas, raspberries, strawberries or peaches.*
- *Serve the risotto with stewed or poached fruits instead, especially rhubarb and apple.*

index